TOP 10 WASHINGTON, DC

RON BURKE
& SUSAN BURKE

DK
EYEWITNESS TRAVEL

Left **Lincoln Memorial** Right **State Dining Room, The White House**

LONDON, NEW YORK,
MELBOURNE, MUNICH AND DELHI
www.dk.com

Produced by Sargasso Media Ltd, London

Printed and bound by South China Printing Co. Ltd, China

First American Edition, 2003
13 14 15 16 10 9 8 7 6 5 4 3 2 1

Published in the United States by DK Publishing, 375 Hudson Street, New York, New York 10014

Reprinted with revisions 2004, 2005, 2006, 2007, 2008, 2009, 2010, 2011, 2012, 2013

Published in the UK by Dorling Kindersley Limited.

A catalog record for this book is available from the Library of Congress

ISSN 1479-344X

ISBN 978-0-75669-665-8

Within each Top 10 list in this book, no hierarchy of quality or popularity is implied. All 10 are, in the editor's opinion, of roughly equal merit.

MIX
Paper from responsible sources
FSC www.fsc.org FSC™ C018179

Contents

Washington, DC's Top 10

The information in this DK Eyewitness Top 10 Travel Guide is checked regularly.

Every effort has been made to ensure that this book is as up-to-date as possible at the time of going to press. Some details, however, such as telephone numbers, opening hours, prices, gallery hanging arrangements and travel information are liable to change. The publishers cannot accept responsibility for any consequences arising from the use of this book, nor for any material on third party websites, and cannot guarantee that any website address in this book will be a suitable source of travel information. We value the views and suggestions of our readers very highly. Please write to: Publisher, DK Eyewitness Travel Guides, Dorling Kindersley, 80 Strand, London WC2R 0RL, or email: travelguides@dk.com.

Cover: Front – **Axiom Photographic Agency:** Tips/Chuck Pefley main; **Dorling Kindersley:** Paul Franklin bl. Spine – **DK Images**: Scott Suchman b. Back – **DK Images**: Kim Sayer c, cl, cr.

Left **Renwick Gallery** Center **US Botanic Garden** Right **Iwo Jima Memorial**

Left **Washington Monument** Right **Red Fox Inn, Middleburg**

Key to abbreviations
Adm *admission charge* **Free** *no admission charge* **Dis. access** *disabled access*

WASHINGTON, DC'S TOP 10

Top 10 Washington, DC's Highlights

A symbol of democracy the world over and the seat of American government, Washington, DC confronts visitors with stirring icons and monuments at every turn. This sparkling self-styled city on the Potomac River is full of marble and light, with beautiful landscaping touches and centuries-old architecture. Built on top of former swampland, Washington was deliberately designed into quadrants, with the US Capitol at its hub. Its many unmissable sights provide unparalleled access to the workings of government, internationally famed museums with priceless exhibits, and the cultural and spiritual foundations of the city and the nation.

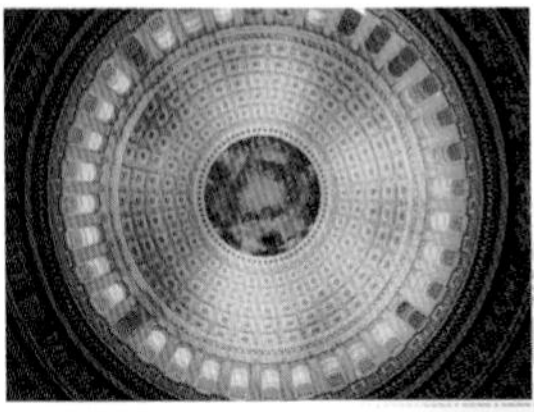

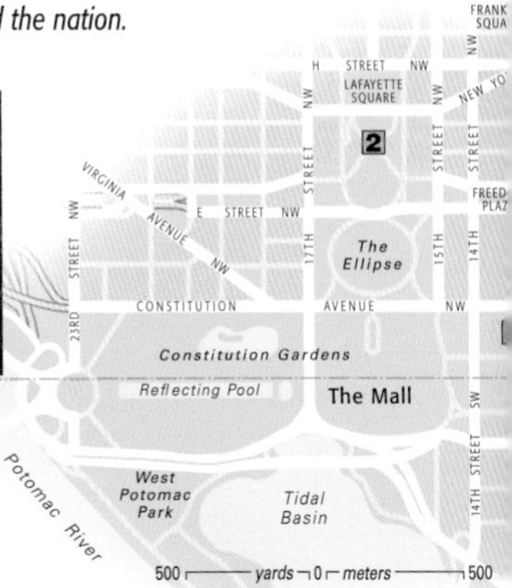

1 United States Capitol

The Capitol's design combines ancient tradition and New World innovation, perfectly invoking the spirit of US democracy *(see pp8–11)*.

2 The White House

The most elegant and familiar of all the world's political residences, the White House has witnessed some of the most consequential decisions of modern history *(see pp12–15)*.

3 National Air and Space Museum

Reportedly the most visited museum in the world, and with good reason. The artifacts of one of mankind's greatest quests – flight above and beyond Earth – are rendered even more impressive by the hangarlike architecture *(see pp16–17)*.

4 National Museum of American History

This museum combines the "America's attic" approach with contemporary exhibits. The artifacts range from political campaign buttons to early locomotives, as well as the Star-Spangled Banner *(see pp18–19)*.

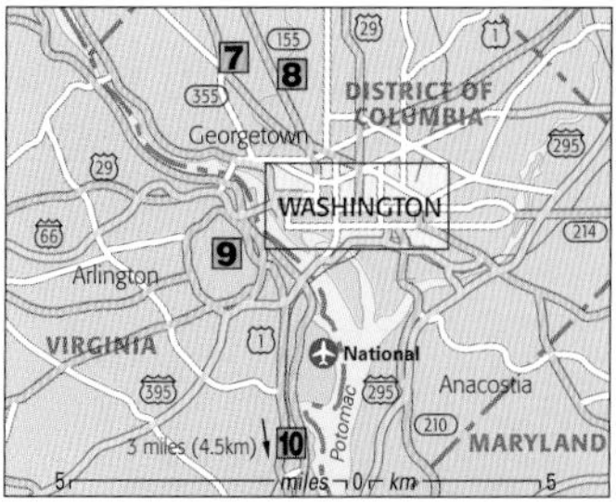

10 Mount Vernon

George Washington's estate and mansion is a perfect example of the gentleman-farmer roots of many of America's founders *(see pp32–5)*.

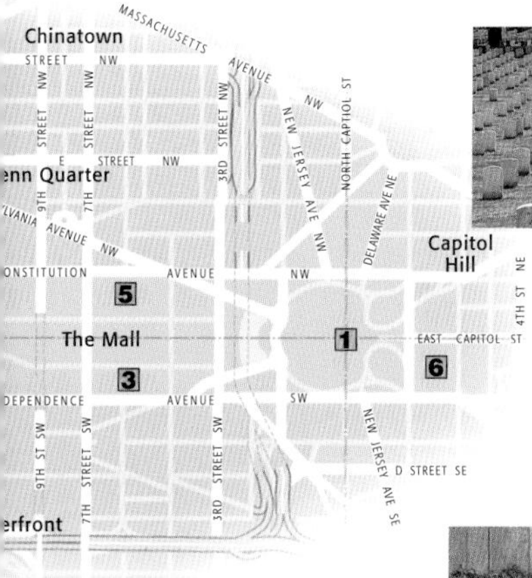

9 Arlington National Cemetery

Four million people each year visit these rolling lawns studded with the headstones of America's war dead. A moving and reflective experience *(see pp30–31)*.

5 National Gallery of Art

The National Gallery's vast collection makes it one of the greatest art museums in the world *(see pp20–23)*.

8 National Zoological Park

Animals from across the world's varied habitats can be seen and learned about at this internationally recognized leader in animal care, breeding of endangered species, and public education *(see pp28–9)*.

6 Library of Congress

The breathtaking interior of the largest library in the world does full justice to its 120 million items, the works fill 530 miles (850 km) of shelves *(see pp24–5)*.

7 Washington National Cathedral

Ancient and modern come together in this "national house of prayer," from the Gothic architecture to the Space Window *(see pp26–7)*.

TOP 10 United States Capitol

From the elevated site that Pierre L'Enfant (see p36) *described as "a pedestal waiting for a monument," the dignified Capitol has stood unwavering as the symbol of American democracy throughout its 200-year history. From the legislative session called by President Jefferson in 1803 to approve the Louisiana Purchase through to the House of Representatives' vote in 1998 to impeach President Clinton, these halls have witnessed an often rough-and-tumble democratic process. The Capitol's frescoes and art collection qualify it as a notable museum, but its millions of tourists come, above all, to brush shoulders with history, both remembered and in the making.*

Façade

The Visitor Center is located underground at the front of the Capitol, facing east. See www.visitthecapitol.gov

The Capitol is most inspiring when viewed rising up from the Mall.

- *National Mall, between 1st and 3rd Sts and Independence and Constitution Aves, SW*
- *Map R5*
- *202-226-8000*
- *www.visitthecapitol.gov*
- *Open 8:30am–4:30pm Mon–Sat*
- *Free (pass required for tours)*

Top 10 Features

1. Capitol Dome
2. Rotunda
3. Senate Chamber
4. House Chamber
5. Old Senate Chamber
6. National Statuary Hall
7. Brumidi Corridors
8. Hall of Columns
9. Columbus Doors
10. West Front

1 Capitol Dome

The central dome *(above)* defines the city for people worldwide. It was added, with the Statue of Freedom *(see p11)*, between 1855 and 1866.

2 Rotunda

America's first president ascends into the heavens in this 4,664-sq ft (430-sq m) fresco *The Apotheosis of Washington*, lining the interior of the dome *(above)*.

3 Senate Chamber

A semicircle of 100 desks faces the dais in this eminent assembly room *(below)*. Democrats sit to the right, Republicans to the left.

For more sights on Capitol Hill **See pp70–73**

4 House Chamber
The largest room in the Capitol is used for daily deliberations of the House of Representatives and for joint meetings of the House and Senate.

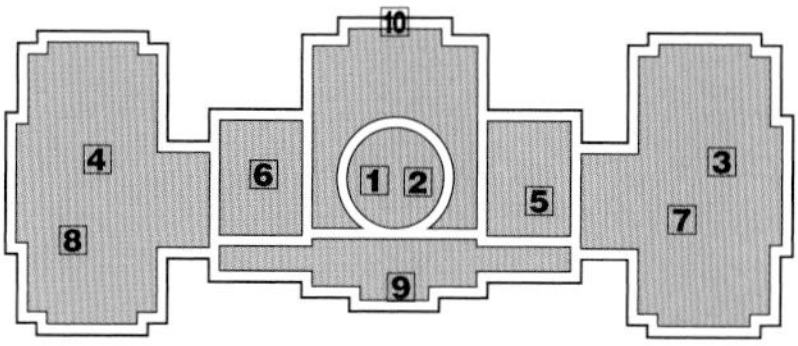

Plan of the US Capitol

5 Old Senate Chamber
Used by the Senate from 1810 to 1859, this chamber witnessed debates on the core issues of the development of the United States.

6 National Statuary Hall
The monumental *Liberty and the Eagle* by Enrico Causici (c.1819) overlooks this hall *(right)* – the original House Chamber.

7 Brumidi Corridors
Constantino Brumidi (1805–80) designed these ornate passageways *(above)* on the lower floor of the Senate wing.

8 Hall of Columns
This striking corridor, more than 100 ft (30 m) long with lofty ceilings, is named after the 28 gracefully fluted white marble columns along its length. It houses additional items from the collection of the original House Chamber.

9 Columbus Doors
These imposing bronze doors, 17 ft (5 m) tall, consist of reliefs picturing Christopher Columbus's life and his discovery of America. Designed by Randolph Rogers, the doors were cast in Munich in 1860.

10 West Front
The west front of the Capitol *(above)*, facing the Mall, is the site of presidential inaugurations, concerts, and other ceremonial events. Its three-part Neo-Classical façade is an expression of bicameral legislature.

Capitol Guide
Current tours cover the historic sections in the center of the building, including the Rotunda, the National Statuary Hall, and the crypt. The galleries of the Senate and House of Representatives Chambers are open to the public when either body is in session. Visitors may obtain gallery passes at the House and Senate Appointment Desk on the upper level of the Visitor Center.

Left **British burn the Capitol, 1814** Right **Charles Bulfinch**

Top 10 Events in the US Capitol's History

1 1787
The US Constitution authorizes the establishment of a federal district to be the seat of the American government.

2 1791
George Washington selects the site for the new Capitol, with his city planner, Pierre Charles L'Enfant, on Jenkins Hill, 88 ft (27 m) above the Potomac River.

3 1792
Dr. William Thornton wins a design contest for "Congress House," in which he proposed a simple central domed hall flanked by two rectangular wings.

4 1800
Congress moves from Philadelphia to occupy the north wing of the Capitol.

George Washington

5 1811
The Capitol is fully occupied by the House of Representatives and Senate, the Supreme Court, and Library of Congress.

6 1814
British troops burn the Capitol during the War of 1812.

7 1818
Charles Bulfinch takes over restoration of the fire-damaged building and supervises its reconstruction. The Senate House and Supreme Court occupy new rooms by 1819 and the Rotunda is first used in 1824 to host a grand reception for General Lafayette.

8 1851
The Capitol is again damaged by fire. It is redesigned and rebuilt once more under the direction of Thomas U. Walter, who designs the cast-iron dome. Work continues on the Dome during the Civil War, while the Capitol is also used as a hospital, barracks, and bakery.

9 1880s–1900
Modern electrical lighting and the first elevator are installed.

10 1958–1962
The east front is extended 32 ft (10 m) east of the old sandstone front. The west front is restored between 1983 and 1987. This work produces the Capitol we see today.

For more moments in Washington, DC's history **See pp36–7**

Top 10 Works of Art in the US Capitol

1. Statue of Freedom, Thomas Crawford (Dome)
2. *The Apotheosis of Washington*, Constantino Brumidi (Rotunda)
3. *General George Washington Resigning His Commission*, John Trumball (Rotunda)
4. Columbus Doors, Randolph Rogers (East Front)
5. Minton Tiles (floors and offices)
6. Brumidi Corridors (Senate Wing)
7. *Statue to Lucretia Mott, Elizabeth Cady Stanton, and Susan B. Anthony*, Adelaide Johnson (Rotunda)
8. Statuary (National Statuary Hall)
9. *Declaration of Independence*, John Trumball (Rotunda)
10. *Baptism of Pocahontas, prior to her marriage to John Rolfe*, Antonio Cappellano (Rotunda)

The American Ideal

Although the Statue of Freedom may appear to face away from the heartland, she is nevertheless the embodiment of all Americans. Standing imperiously over the capital, and the nation as a whole, she encapsulates the notion of freedom for all citizens, laid out in the US Constitution. It is an ideal still fiercely protected today.

The Statue of Freedom

Crowning the Capitol dome stands Thomas Crawford's Statue of Freedom, commissioned in 1855, and, according to Capitol police officers, the figure is the most common subject of visitors' questions. Why does it face to the east, away from the nation? Freedom is depicted as a classical female figure, draped in flowing robes. Her Roman helmet, however, features the crest of an eagle's head, feathers, and talons, which some believe to be a reference to Native American dress. Crawford substituted the Roman helmet for the original liberty cap, a symbol of freed slaves, when the then US Secretary of War, Jefferson Davis, objected. The statue faces east in accordance with the front of the building, not the rest of the country. The east front was made the main building entrance simply because it faces an approach of level ground. This monumental symbol of liberty is 19.5 ft (6 m) tall and weighs around 15,000 lbs (6,800 kg). Sadly Crawford died in 1857, before it was erected.

TOP 10 The White House

Possibly the most famous residential landmark in the world, this dramatic Neo-Classical mansion has been the residence of the US president and family, the seat of executive power, and a working office building for over 200 years. Situated at the nation's most recognizable address, 1600 Pennsylvania Avenue, the White House reflects the power of the presidency. Its 132 rooms preserve and display the cultural settings of America's past and present. Lafayette Park to the north and the Ellipse to the south are popular sites for viewing this American icon.

North façade

If you have a telephoto lens or binoculars, the carved floral decorations on the north entrance and the plantings of the Rose Garden, viewed from the Ellipse, deserve attention.

The White House has no public restrooms. The nearest facilities are at the Visitor Center and the Ellipse Visitor Pavilion, near 15th and E streets NW.

- *1600 Pennsylvania Ave, NW (Visitor Center: 1450 Pennsylvania Ave, NW)*
- *Map N4*
- *202-208-1631*
- *www.whitehouse.gov*
- *Current information about tours can be obtained at 202-456-7041*
- *Free*
- *Dis. access*

Top 10 Features

1. North Façade
2. South Façade
3. Oval Office
4. West Wing
5. East Room
6. Blue Room
7. Map Room
8. State Dining Room
9. Lincoln Bedroom
10. Visitor Center

1 North Façade

The stately but welcoming main entrance on Pennsylvania Avenue has a beautifully proportioned Ionic portico, added in 1829. Painted Virginia sandstone gives the building its white luster.

2 South Façade

The large semicircular portico added in 1824 dominates the south view. The six main columns create an optical illusion, appearing to stretch from ground to roofline, emphasizing the classical proportions.

3 Oval Office

This illustrious room *(above)* is the setting for the president's core tasks. Each leader adds his own touch – Barack Obama has added a bust of Martin Luther King, Jr and Native American pottery.

4 West Wing

This wing is the executive operational center of the White House, moved here in 1902 to allow more privacy in the main building.

5 East Room

The East Room *(left)* has been used chiefly for large entertainment or ceremonial gatherings, such as dances, award presentations, press conferences, and historic bill signings.

For more sights around the White House **See pp90–93**

6 Blue Room
The Blue Room *(above)* is the most elegant of all the reception rooms - it was George Washington who suggested its oval shape.

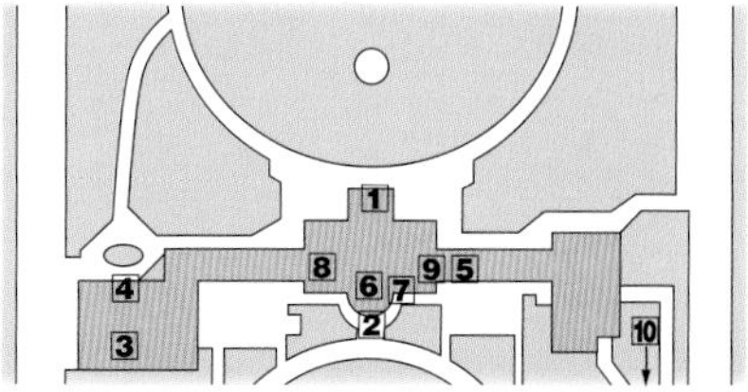

Plan of the White House

10 Visitor Center
The White House Visitor Center *(above)* has engrossing exhibits on various aspects of the mansion. It also offers park ranger talks, a souvenir shop, and special events such as military band concerts.

7 Map Room
Graceful Chippendale pieces furnish this private meeting room. Franklin D. Roosevelt adapted it as his situation room to assess the progress of World War II.

8 State Dining Room
As many as 140 guests may enjoy the president's hospitality in this formal dining room *(below)*.

9 Lincoln Bedroom
Although the name for this room is a misnomer – Abraham Lincoln used it as an office – a number of his possessions can be found here. Mary Todd Lincoln bought the imposing Victorian bed *(above)*, made of carved rosewood, in 1861.

Designing the White House

George Washington personally supervised the design and construction of the White House, although he never lived here. John and Abigail Adams became its first residents in 1800. At the same time, the seat of government was moved from Philadelphia to Washington, D.C. After the British burned the White House in 1814, it became the responsibility of the James Monroe presidency to redecorate. Much of what is seen today reflects Monroe's taste.

Left **Vermeil Room** Right **Diplomatic Reception Room**

White House Decorative Features

1 The Vermeil Room
"Vermeil" refers to the collection of gilded objects by early 19th-century silversmiths on display. Portraits of several First Ladies adorn the walls, and the room is grounded by one of the Empire-style tables purchased by President Andrew Jackson in 1829 for use in the East Room.

2 China Room Collection
The White House collection of china services had grown so large by 1917 that Mrs Woodrow Wilson set aside a room in which to display it. State and family china belonging to nearly every US president fills the fine display cabinets.

3 Grand Staircase
Descending to the Central Hall on the north side, the Grand Staircase is used for ceremonial entrances to state events in the East Room. Portraits of 20th-century presidents line the stairwell.

4 Library
This former storage room was turned into a library in 1935, and contains a collection of books intended to reflect the philosophical and practical aspects of the presidency. Many pieces of the furniture in this room are attributed to the cabinetmaker Duncan Phyfe.

Grand Staircase

5 Diplomatic Reception Room Wallpaper
The panoramic wallpaper is a series of large "Views of North America" printed in France in 1834.

6 Lighter Relieving a Steamboat Aground
This 1847 painting in the Green Room, by George Caleb Bingham, conveys the vitality of the nation.

7 Sand Dunes at Sunset, Atlantic City
This beach landscape (c.1885) by Henry Ossawa Tanner was the first work by an African American to be hung in the White House.

8 North Entrance Carvings
Scottish stonemasons created the carved surround for the north doorway with flowing garlands of roses and acorns.

9 Monroe Plateau
James Monroe ordered a gilt table service from France in 1817. The plateau centerpiece is an impressive 14.5 ft (4.5 m) long when fully extended.

10 Seymour Tall-Case Clock
This Oval Office clock ticks so loudly that its pendulum must be stopped when television broadcasts originate from the room.

Top 10 Events in The White House's History

1. George Washington supervises construction (1792)
2. John and Abigail Adams move in (1800)
3. The Lewis and Clark expedition to the North-west is planned (1803)
4. The British burn the White House (1814)
5. James Monroe moves into the partially rebuilt residence (1817)
6. The Executive Mansion is renamed the "White House" (1901)
7. President Roosevelt's World War II "Fireside Chats" inform and inspire Americans
8. Jackie Kennedy restores the house (1961–2)
9. Nixon announces his resignation (Aug 8, 1974)
10. Barack Obama becomes first African-American President (2009)

President Truman's Renovations

From the time Harry S. Truman moved into the White House, he had noticed signs that the building was under a great deal of stress: "The floors pop and the drapes move back and forth," and "[t]he damned place is haunted, sure as shootin'." In 1948, after some investigation, engineers confirmed that it was structural weakness, not ghosts, that was causing the problems. Some people said the house was standing "only from force of habit." The only certain solution was to move the Truman family to nearby Blair House and completely rebuild the White House within its external walls. Contractors gutted the inside of the building in its entirety. Workers then built a steel frame, similar to those found in large office buildings, inside the remaining shell. Within the frame, the White House was recreated, room by room, from scratch, but in keeping with the original design. Most structural elements that can be seen today were built between 1948 and 1952, although a few earlier elements had been carefully dismantled and re-installed during reconstruction. America's three major networks broadcast the first-ever television tour of the residence in 1952. President Truman himself proudly led the tour and even entertained viewers by playing a tune on one of the pianos in the East Room (see p12)*. A decade later, that arbiter of style Jacqueline Kennedy again restored many of the period features.*

The White House gutted in 1948

TOP 10 National Air and Space Museum

This fascinating museum's 22 main exhibition galleries pay homage to some of the most ingenious and beautifully crafted objects of flight, from the Wright brothers' airplane to powerful spacecraft. America by Air outlines the history of America's airline industry including airplanes from the formative years of mechanical flight. Compelling exhibitions put these historic objects in their social and political context. Moon rock is displayed so that the public can touch it.

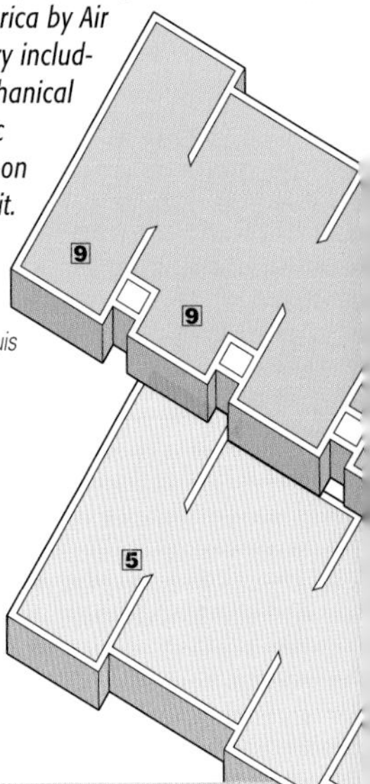

Museum façade

McDonald's, Boston Market, and Donato's Pizzeria are located in the greenhouse-like extension on the east end of the building.

The museum features in the film *Night At The Museum: Battle of the Smithsonian*, starring actor Ben Stiller, released in the summer of 2009.

- *Independence Ave, 6th St, SW*
- *Map Q5*
- *202-633-1000*
- *www.nasm.si.edu*
- *Open 10am–5:30pm daily; closed Dec 25*
- *Dis. access*
- *Museum: Free; Planetarium and theater shows: adults (13–59 years) $9.00, seniors (over 60 years) $8.00, youths (2–12 years) $7.50, Smithsonian members $6.50*
- *Steven F. Udvar-Hazy Center: Dulles International Airport*

Top 10 Exhibits

1. 1903 Wright *Flyer*
2. Ryan NYP *Spirit of St. Louis*
3. Apollo 11 Command Module *Columbia*
4. Amelia Earhart's Lockheed Vega
5. Skylab Orbital Workshop
6. How Things Fly
7. Looking at Earth
8. Moving Beyond Earth
9. WWI and WWII Aviation
10. Steven F. Udvar-Hazy Center

1 1903 Wright Flyer

On December 17, 1903, Orville Wright flew this craft *(above)* 120 ft (35 m), making it the first powered, piloted plane to be airborne. Muslin on a spruce and ash frame provided a light but strong body. The Wright brothers also designed the engine.

3 Apollo 11 Command Module Columbia

This vessel was the command center for the first lunar landing. It carried Neil Armstrong, Michael Collins, and "Buzz" Aldrin to the Moon and back.

2 Ryan NYP Spirit of St. Louis

Charles Lindbergh flew this plane *(below)* on the first solo transatlantic flight, 3,610 miles (5,810 km) from Long Island to Paris in 1927. His 33-hour flight made him one of the most famous men of his age and turned aviation into a public craze. NYP stands for New York–Paris.

For more museums in Washington, DC **See pp42–3**

4 Amelia Earhart's Lockheed 5B Vega

In this striking airplane *(above)*, Amelia Earhart completed the second solo nonstop flight across the Atlantic, from Newfoundland to Ireland in 14 hours, 54 minutes.

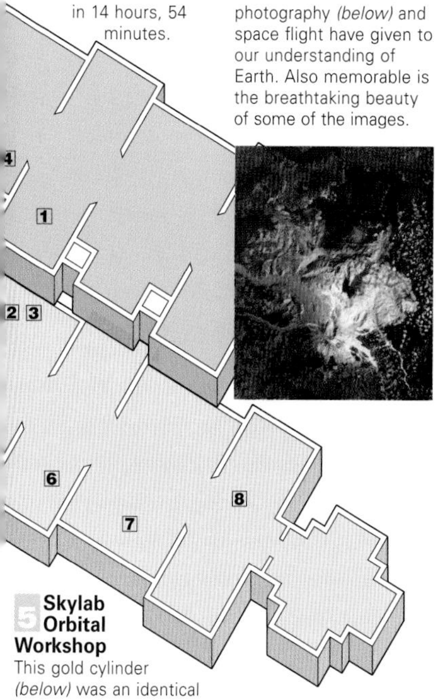

5 Skylab Orbital Workshop

This gold cylinder *(below)* was an identical backup to the workshop that provided living and research space for the first US space station.

6 How Things Fly

Hands-on exhibits here lead visitors through the basics of flight, both human and animal, and explain forces that control flight of all types, from a helium balloon to a mission to Mars.

7 Looking at Earth

The focus here is on the contribution aerial photography *(below)* and space flight have given to our understanding of Earth. Also memorable is the breathtaking beauty of some of the images.

8 Moving Beyond Earth

This exhibition explores the history and importance of human spaceflight in the United States during the space shuttle and space station era, interpreting the story of human spaceflight through artifacts, immersive experiences, high-technology interactive kiosks, and a Presentation Center.

9 WWI and WWII Aviation

A collection of Allied and Axis planes from World Wars I *(below)* and II, such as the Messerschmitt Bf 109 and the Supermarine Spitfire, makes this one of the most popular parts of the museum.

10 Steven F. Udvar-Hazy Center

This aviation area near Washington Dulles International Airport consists of two exhibition hangars. Opened to celebrate the 100th anniversary of the Wright brothers' first powered flight, it displays nearly 300 aircraft and spacecraft, including the space shuttle Discovery.

Key

First Floor

Second Floor

Museum Guide

Entrances to the museum are on both Independence Avenue and the Mall. Both lead into the spacious central hall where the most famous airplanes of all time are displayed. An information booth is near the Independence Avenue entrance. Visitors who plan to enjoy a film at the Lockheed Martin IMAX Theater or the Albert Einstein Planetarium can obtain their tickets on arrival at the museum, or buy them online, prior to their visit.

TOP 10 National Museum of American History

Three huge floors filled with a variety of fascinating objects make up this paean to American culture. The first floor focuses on science and technology, including hands-on experiments and exhibitions on transport, electricity, and machinery. The second floor is home to the famous Star-Spangled Banner, while the third floor features a stirring tribute to the American presidency and military history. The museum is undergoing major renovation work, which is ongoing in phases. Call ahead or check the website for information on the latest exhibitions.

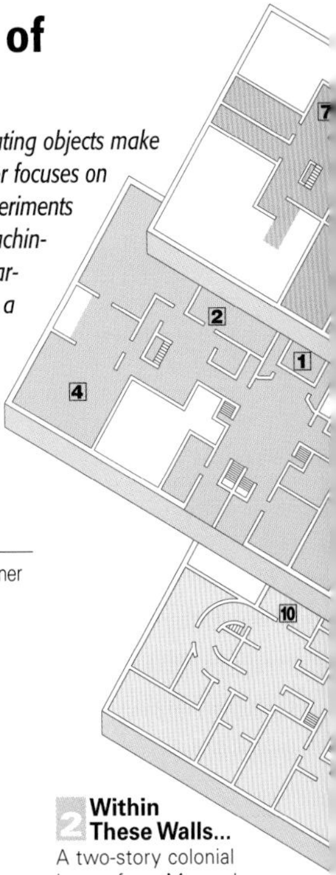

Façade

The Stars and Stripes Café and Constitution Café are located within the museum and offer a variety of sweet and savory treats.

- *14th St and Constitution Ave, NW*
- *Map P4*
- *202-633-1000*
- *www.americanhistory.si.edu/*
- *Open 10am–5:30pm daily; extended hours in summer (see website for details); closed Dec 25*
- *Dis. access*
- *Free*

Top 10 Exhibits

1. The Star-Spangled Banner
2. Within These Walls...
3. The Price of Freedom: Americans at War
4. The First Ladies at the Smithsonian
5. John Bull Locomotive
6. America on the Move
7. National Treasures of Popular Culture
8. Gunboat Philadelphia
9. The American Presidency
10. Invention At Play

1 The Star-Spangled Banner

The flag that inspired the national anthem *(below)* is strikingly large – originally 30 by 42 ft (9 by 13 m) – although timeworn. Created by Baltimore flagmaker Mary Pickersgill in 1813, it is on display in the gallery, which recreates the Battle of Baltimore and the burning of the White House.

2 Within These Walls...

A two-story colonial house from Massachusetts has been rebuilt within the museum, to explore the 200-year history of the families who lived there *(below)*.

3 The Price of Freedom: Americans at War

This gallery explores the nation's military history, from the French and Indian War in the 1750s to recent conflicts in Afghanistan and Iraq. The exhibition features a Vietnam-era Huey helicopter and a World War II jeep.

For moments in the history of Washington, DC **See pp36–7**

Key

First Floor

Second Floor

Third Floor

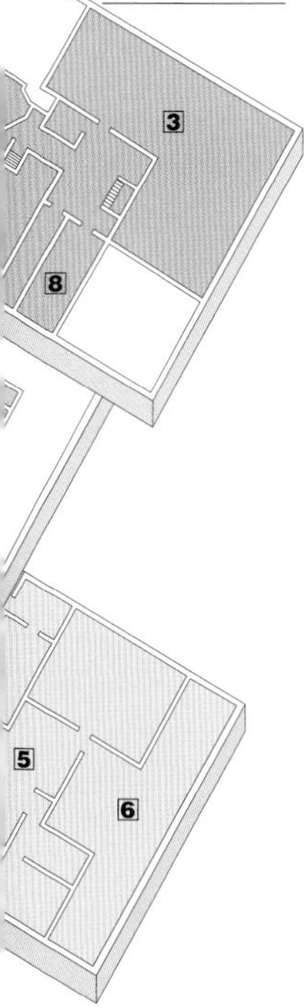

4 The First Ladies at the Smithsonian

The First Ladies' gallery is a firm favorite and includes inaugural gowns worn by Jackie Kennedy, Eleanor Roosevelt, Nancy Reagan *(below)*, and Michelle Obama.

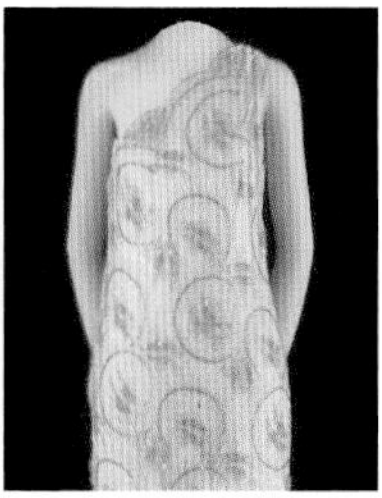

5 John Bull Locomotive

The oldest still-operable, self-propelled vehicle in the world, the John Bull locomotive was built in England and brought to America in 1831. The only one of its kind, it transported passengers between Philadelphia and New York on the Camden and Amboy Railroad between 1831 and 1866.

6 America on the Move

Multimedia presentations and other theatrical techniques tell the story of America's transportation since 1876, including this 1950 Buick Super sedan *(below)*. The vast exhibition holds over 340 objects.

7 National Treasures of Popular Culture

Wonderful artifacts from the world of popular entertainment, including Dorothy's ruby slippers from *The Wizard of Oz*, a Kermit the Frog puppet, and other favorites from the worlds of entertainment and sports.

8 Gunboat Philadelphia

In October 1776, the *Philadelphia* was sunk by the British during a battle on Lake Champlain in New York, and rested on the bottom of the lake until it was recovered in 1935. It came to the museum in 1964, complete with its equipment and the 24-pound ball that sent the gunboat to the bottom.

9 The American Presidency

The portable desk Thomas Jefferson used to write the Declaration of Independence and the top hat *(above)* Abraham Lincoln was wearing the night he was assassinated are highlights of this exhibition featuring hundreds of objects from the presidential office.

10 Invention At Play

A highly interactive gallery for families that aims to show the connection between play and invention. Kids will enjoy "meeting" the inventors and learning to sail on a sailboard simulator.

Museum Events

An amazing variety of events, both entertaining and enlightening, are available to the public. Phone ahead or check online for updates. Try out some of the interactive exhibits, or take part in debates on controversial issues. It includes a section of the original Woolworth's lunch counter from Greensboro, NC, a landmark from the Civil Rights Movement, when African-Americans sat at this "whites only" counter asking to be served. At regular intervals you are invited to relive the events of 1960.

TOP 10 National Gallery of Art

The collections at this immense gallery rival those of any art museum in the world, displaying milestones of western art from the Middle Ages through to the 20th century and including Italian Renaissance works, Dutch Masters, French Impressionists, and all ages of American art. John Russell Pope designed the harmonious Neo-Classical West Building in 1941. The East Building is the work of architect I.M. Pei, and it is often considered a work of art in itself.

East Building

The Cascade Café, on the concourse between the West and East Buildings, has an espresso bar, while the Pavillion Café in the Sculpture Garden is an elegant spot to grab a bite.

The courts on the main floor of the West Building are a wonderful place to relax, away from the stream of tourists.

- *3rd–7th Sts at Constitution Avenue NW*
- *Map Q4*
- *202-737-4215*
- *www.nga.gov*
- *Open 10am–5pm Mon–Sat, 11am–6pm Sun; closed Dec 25, Jan 1*
- *Free*
- *Dis. access*

Top 10 Paintings

1. Ginevra de' Benci
2. The Adoration of the Magi
3. Girl with the Red Hat
4. The Alba Madonna
5. Watson and the Shark
6. Portraits of the First Five Presidents
7. Wivenhoe Park, Essex
8. The River of Light
9. Right and Left
10. Number 1, 1950 (Lavender Mist)

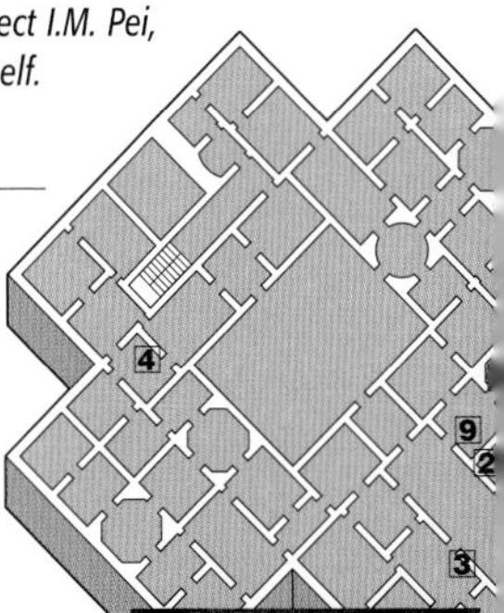

1 Ginevra de' Benci

The careful modeling of lustrous flesh against juniper foliage make this Leonardo da Vinci canvas of 1474, his only one in the US, a lively but composed work *(above)*.

2 The Adoration of the Magi

This festive view of the Magi at Christ's birthplace *(right)* was painted in tempura on a circular panel by Fra Angelico and Filippo Lippi in about 1445.

3 Girl with the Red Hat

This 1665 portrait *(above)* shows off Johannes Vermeer's striking use of color: yellow highlights in the blue robe, purple under the hat, turquoise in the eyes. The luminosity is enhanced by the smooth panel base.

4 The Alba Madonna

Unusually, the Madonna in Raphael's 1510 work is shown seated on the ground. The composition is serene, but it shows Christ accepting the cross from St John the Baptist, a precursor of events to come.

5 Watson and the Shark

The sensational subject matter, muscular painting, and expressions of dread and anxiety made this John Singleton Copley painting shocking when it was first displayed in 1778.

7 Wivenhoe Park, Essex

Light and shade, the perception of calm, and clarity of detail create an absorbing and soothing landscape *(above)*. In this 1816 work John Constable demonstrates his love of the English countryside.

8 The River of Light

Frederick Edwin Church's 1877 oil painting of the Amazon is based on sketches taken during a trip to South America. The painting radiates an otherworldly air and emphasizes the power of nature.

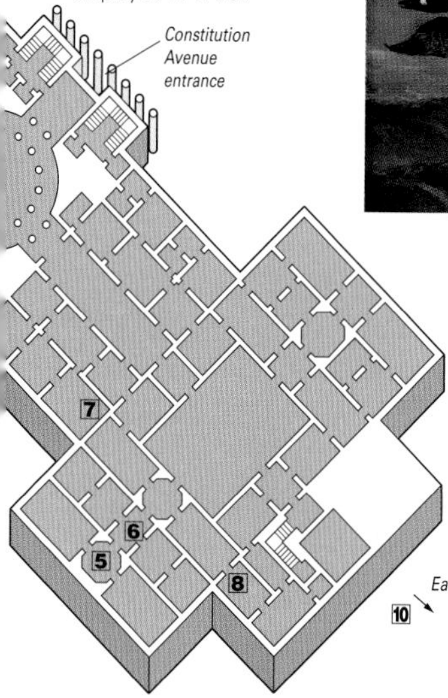

9 Right and Left

The title of Winslow Homer's 1909 painting *(above)* refers to shooting ducks with separate barrels of a shotgun. The fleeting nature of the ducks' existence echoes our own.

10 Number 1, 1950 (Lavender Mist)

This Jackson Pollock composition is a monument of America's emergence as a center of art innovation (1950).

6 Portraits of the First Five Presidents

This is the only complete set of Gilbert Stuart's paintings of the first five presidents (1817–21), including George Washington *(right)*, still in existence. Sadly another set was partially destroyed by fire in 1851 at the Library of Congress.

Gallery Guide

The first floor contains European paintings and sculpture, and American art. The ground floor displays works on paper, sculpture, decorative arts, and temporary exhibits. The location of works changes periodically. An underground concourse leads to the East Building.

Left **Salem Cove, Prendergast** Center **Japanese Footbridge, Monet** Right **The East Building**

National Gallery of Art Collections

Collections Floorplan

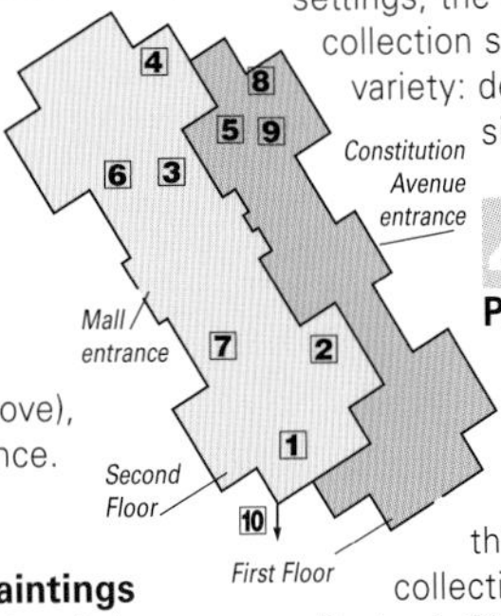

1 American Paintings

The breadth of this collection reveals many themes: portraiture, a desire for accuracy in depicting American life and landscape (see *Salem Cove*, above), and a social conscience.

2 French 19th-century Paintings

Especially rich in works of the Impressionists, this collection includes some of the world's most beloved works of art, like Monet's *Japanese Footbridge* or Degas' *Four Dancers*.

3 Italian 13th- to 15th-century Paintings

Best known for the increasing mastery of the naturalistic portrayal of the human figure and of interior and exterior settings, the works in this collection still have appealing variety: decorative, mystical, simple, and elegant.

4 Italian 16th-century Painting

The mature flowering of the Renaissance bursts forth in this deep and broad collection of works by Raphael, Giorgione, Titian, and many others.

5 Works on Paper

The National Gallery is especially strong in this area. Repeat visitors see an almost unbelievable quantity and variety of exquisite drawings, prints, illustrated books, and photographs. The permanent collection contains more than 65,000 items, dating as far back as the 11th century.

6 Dutch and Flemish Paintings

Again, visitors will find an overwhelmingly rich array of Old Master works by artists such as Rembrandt, Frans Hals, Van Dyck, Rubens, Vermeer, and their contemporaries.

7 Spanish Paintings

El Greco, Zurbarán, Murillo, and Velázquez are just some of the 18th- to 19th-century highlights in this vibrant collection.

Portrait of an Elderly Lady, Frans Hals

For more art galleries in Washington, DC **See pp40–41**

8 Decorative Arts
Sumptuous tapestries, full of imagery, outstanding pieces of furniture, and everyday items such as plates and bowls, give a wonderful glimpse of the passing centuries in Europe.

9 European Sculpture
Portrait busts and portrait medals have always been important products of the sculptor's studio, and many fine examples are displayed here. There is also an especially absorbing look at Rodin and some experimental sculptural pieces by Degas.

10 Painting and Sculpture of the 20th Century
The frantic rate of change in 20th-century art is laid out here. From Matisse's Fauvist works, the Cubists Picasso and Braque, the abstraction of Mondrian, Surrealists such as Magritte and Miró, high Modernists David Smith, and Mark Rothko, right up to minimalism and Pop Art.

Top 10 Works in the Sculpture Garden

1. *Puellae (Girls)*, Magdalena Abakanowicz (1992)
2. *House I*, Roy Lichtenstein (1996–8)
3. *Four-Sided Pyramid*, Sol LeWitt (1997)
4. *Graft*, Roxy Paine (2008)
5. *Personnage Gothique, Oiseau-Éclair*, Joan Miró (1974)
6. *Six-Part Seating*, Scott Burton (1985–98)
7. *Spider*, Louise Bourgeois (1996)
8. *Thinker on a Rock*, Barry Flanagan (1997)
9. *Chair Transformation Number 20B*, Lucas Samaras (1996)
10. *Moondog*, Tony Smith (1964–99)

The East Building and Sculpture Garden

The East Building is an angular construction designed to house permanent and touring exhibitions of contemporary art. Its entrance is from 4th Street or from the underground concourse leading from the West Building. A huge orange-and-black mobile by Alexander Calder dominates the lobby, while provocative exhibition halls line the outer walls of the upper halls, connected by spectacular hanging crosswalks. The Sculpture Garden is a wonderful, lively public space integrating contemporary art with beautifully landscaped gardens and a relaxing reflection pool with its spraying central fountain. Located in the six-acre block next to the West Building, the garden includes plantings of native species of trees, shrubs, and perennials, along with 17 pieces from the Gallery's collection and several items on loan from other museums. There are free jazz concerts in the summer on Fridays and the pool transforms into a popular ice-skating rink in winter.

Graft
This work by Roxy Paine was added to the Sculpture Garden in 2008. The huge stainless-steel structure presents two trees, one gnarled and the other smooth, joined to the same trunk.

Top 10 Library of Congress

The focus of this immense library – the greatest accumulation of information and images in the world – is the magnificent Jefferson Building. Its main reading room is one of the most captivating spaces in the city. Collections encompass many subjects – the law library is especially notable, as are materials and books relating to Africa, the Middle East, and the rest of the world. In addition there are collections of comic books, jazz recordings and memorabilia, photography, films, and television broadcasts. The Adams and Madison buildings are more recent additions.

Façade

Free standby tickets are often available for concerts, from 6:30pm for 8pm performances and 12:30pm for 2pm performances.

For visitors wishing to use the library for research, reader cards can be obtained on the same day by applying at Room LM 140 in the Madison Building.

- *1st St, SE, between Independence Ave and E Capitol St*
- *Map S5*
- *202-707-8000*
- *www.loc.gov*
- *Open 8:30am–4:30pm Mon–Sat; James Madison Building: 8:30am–9:30pm Mon–Fri, to 5pm Sat; John Adams Building: 8:30am–9:30pm Mon, Wed & Thu; to 5pm Tue, Fri & Sat*
- *Dis. access*
- *Free* • *For advance concert tickets phone 800-551-7328 or visit www.ticketmaster.com*

Top 10 Features

1. Exterior
2. Main Reading Room
3. Great Hall
4. Gutenberg Bible
5. Creating the United States
6. African and Middle Eastern Reading Room
7. Mosaic of Minerva
8. Concert Series
9. America Map
10. Neptune Fountain

1 Exterior

Congress authorized the construction of a new library building in the style of the Italian Renaissance in 1886. Its plan reflects that of the Capitol – two wings with a central dome. The portico contains busts of nine "great men of literature" from Demosthenes to Washington Irving.

2 Main Reading Room

In this splendid room *(above)* the civilized arts are represented by allegorical figures atop its eight giant columns: Religion, History, Commerce, Art, Philosophy, Poetry, Law, and Science.

3 Great Hall

The ceiling, resplendent with stained-glass skylights, soars 75 ft (20 m) above the beautiful marble floor. Ceremonial staircases *(left)* at either end of the hall are elaborately carved with scenes of cherubs engaged in making music, catching butterflies, and using the newly invented telephone.

4 Gutenberg Bible
This superb example of the first book printed with movable type *(right)* is one of only three perfect vellum copies to survive. Also here is the handwritten Giant Bible of Mainz.

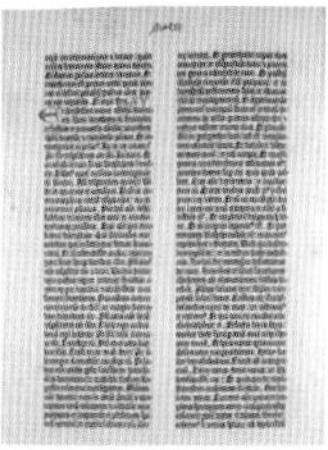

5 Creating the United States
Explore the creative process through which the nation was born. Innovative technology reveals how drafts of the Declaration of Independence, the Constitution, and the Bill of Rights were forged out of invention, insight, collaboration, and compromise.

6 African and Middle Eastern Reading Room
This long room, for research work on this ancient geographical area, is one of 21 that give users access to the special collections.

Key

▒	First Floor
▒	Second Floor
▒	Third Floor

7 Mosaic of Minerva
A beautiful marble mosaic of Minerva overlooks the staircase near the Visitors' Gallery *(below)*.

8 Concert Series
The Coolidge Auditorium hosts a range of performances: solo, trio, and quartet programs; classical song; period instrument ensembles; jazz, folk, gospel, and pop. Concerts are free; tickets through Ticketmaster.

9 America Map
In the exhibition "Exploring the Early Americas", see the 1507 Waldseemüller map, the first map to use the word "America". Also view pre-Columbian artifacts.

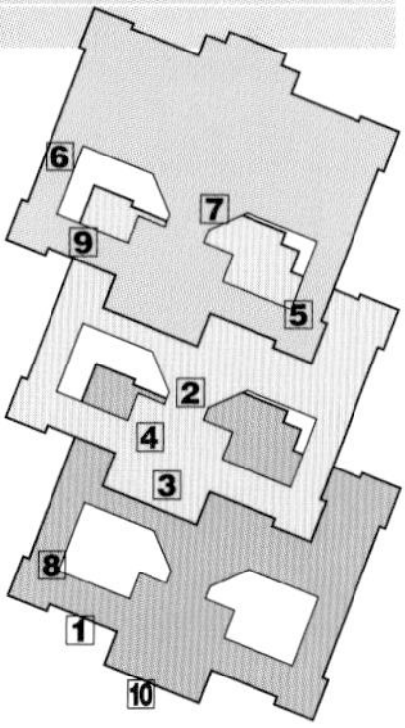

Library of Congress Floorplan

10 Neptune Fountain
Roland Hinton Perry sculpted this dashing tribute to the god Neptune and his court *(above)*, installed in 1898 in front of the Jefferson Building.

Jefferson's Collection

The library had humble beginnings of just 728 books and three maps, but these were destroyed when the British burned the Capitol building, then home to the library, in 1814. Congress appropriated $23,950 to buy Thomas Jefferson's personal library of 6,487 volumes as the core of a new collection. Another fire in 1851 destroyed many of the books. It has been a goal of the library to replace Jefferson's books with period copies, and today only 282 are still missing.

A Reader's Card is required to enter the Reading Rooms and can be easily obtained in the Madison Building

Washington National Cathedral

This famous Gothic building is the focus of public spiritual life. The structure – the sixth largest cathedral in the world – was completed in 1990, with a 10-story-high nave and a central tower 676 ft (206 m) tall, the highest point in the District of Columbia. This Episcopal church, officially named the Cathedral Church of Saint Peter and Saint Paul, will be undergoing renovations until 2016 following earthquake damage.

Exterior

Live music is a vital part of the life of the Cathedral. Throughout the year, the Cathedral offers concerts, organ and carillon recitals, and live demonstrations. Music is integral to most worship services.

Binoculars or a telephoto lens are a must for appreciating the gargoyles.

- *Massachusetts & Wisconsin Aves NW*
- *Map H4*
- *202-537-6200*
- *www.nationalcathedral.org*
- *Open 10am–5:30pm Mon–Fri, 10am–4pm Sat, 7:45am–4pm Sun (weekend hours subject to change for special events)*
- *Donation*
- *Dis. access*

Top 10 Features

1. Exterior
2. Main Entrance and Creation
3. High Altar
4. Space Window
5. Nave
6. South Rose Window
7. Children's Chapel
8. Gargoyles
9. Pipe Organ
10. Gardens

1 Exterior

The architecture of the cathedral is predominantly English Gothic, created using authentic methods preserved since the Middle Ages, including a cross-shaped floorplan, flying buttresses, and multispired towers.

2 Main Entrance and Creation

The west entrance *(above)* is centered within a high Gothic arch containing a lovely rose window. Above the bronze double doors is *"Ex Nihilo,"* a relief sculpture by Frederick Hart portraying the creation of humankind from chaos.

3 High Altar

The imposing high altar at the east end of the nave *(below)* is made from stone dug from Solomon's quarry outside Jerusalem; the altar is also called the Jerusalem Altar.

4 Space Window

This stained-glass window is notable for commemorating mankind's 20th-century moon landing *(right)*. A piece of moon rock, brought back by Apollo 11 astronauts, is embedded in it.

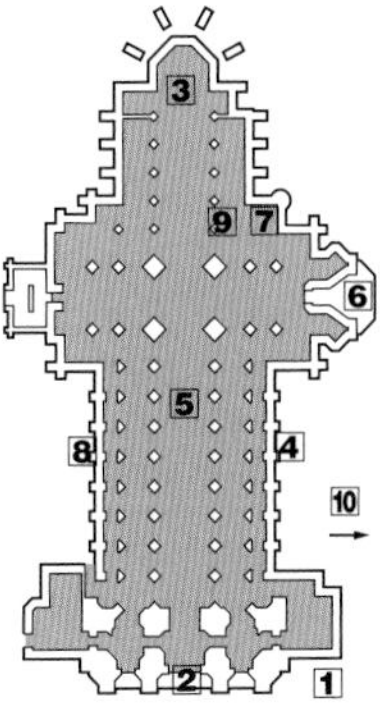

Cathedral Floorplan

7 Children's Chapel

This endearing room is child-scaled with a miniature organ and altar and chairs to fit six-year-olds. Jesus is also shown as a boy in the sculpture here *(below)*.

8 Gargoyles and Grotesques

Derived from decorated spouts on European buildings, these carved ornaments have been given free rein at the cathedral. The 112 carvings include Darth Vader of *Star Wars*® fame and a predatory-looking snake.

5 Nave

The vertical impression given by the nave *(above)* is also typical of English Gothic style. Flags of the states are often displayed around the outer walls.

9 Pipe Organ

This magnificent Aeolian-Skinner instrument has 10,650 pipes. On most Mondays and Wednesdays at 12:30pm, an organist gives a presentation and then demonstrates with a recital.

6 South Rose Window

"The Church Triumphant" is the theme of this elegant stained-glass window *(right)*. The design of Joseph G. Reynolds incorporates 12 brilliantly colored "petals" and numerous other figures.

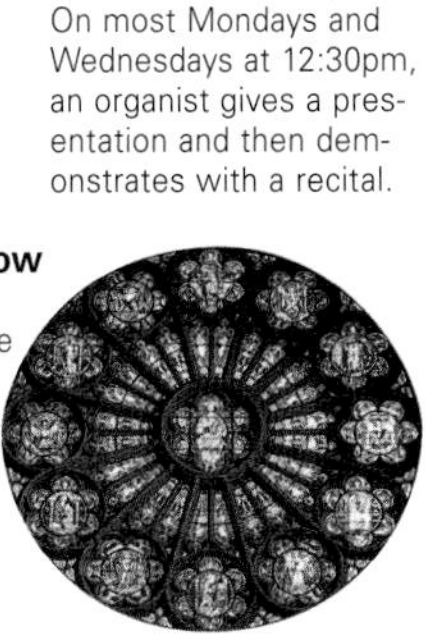

10 Gardens

A medieval walled garden is the model for the cathedral's beautiful Bishop's Garden on the south side of the church. The herb gardens are a delight to the nose as well as the eye: all the stones here originated in a quarry that George Washington once owned.

Building the Cathedral

In 1893 Congress granted a charter to construct Washington National Cathedral. Theodore Roosevelt attended the laying of the foundation stone at the commanding Mount St. Albans location in 1907. The completion of the west towers in 1990 marked the end of 83 years of continuous work. The cathedral is built by the "stone-on-stone" method, using no structural steel. Many architects, including Henry Vaughan, Philip Frohman, and George Bodley, came together to create this inspiring monument. It was built entirely from donations.

Top 10 National Zoological Park

One of the most visited destinations in Washington, the Smithsonian's National Zoo is a beautifully landscaped 163-acre (66-ha) urban park and an innovative center for animal care and conservation. Children and adults delight at seeing rare giant pandas, endangered Asian elephants, and majestic tigers. More than 2,000 animals live here, increasingly housed in habitats that allow natural behavior. The zoo, which opened in 1889, was one of the first in the world to be founded partly with the goal of preserving endangered species.

Entrance sign

Most children's tour groups arrive between 10am and noon in the fall. If you wish to see the popular giant pandas, visit after 2pm when the lines tend to be shorter.

- *3001 Connecticut Ave, NW*
- *Map J4*
- *202-633-4888*
- *www.nationalzoo.si.edu*
- *Open Apr–Oct: grounds 6am–8pm, buildings 10am–6pm daily; Nov–Apr: grounds 6am–6pm, buildings 10am–4:30pm daily; closed Dec 25*
- *From Jun–Sep, the zoo runs its Snore and Roar sleepover events, allowing visitors to take a nocturnal tour and camp in the zoo grounds*
- *Dis. access*
- *Free*

Top 10 Features

1. Giant Pandas
2. Great Cats
3. Asian Elephants
4. Bird House
5. Invertebrate Exhibit
6. Cheetah Conservation Station
7. Amazonia
8. Asia Trail
9. Reptile Discovery Center
10. Great Apes

1 Giant Pandas

Mei Xiang and Tian Tian, two giant pandas on loan from China, made their first appearance at the zoo in 2001 as part of a research and conservation program. Their lively curiosity, social interactions, and physical beauty are fascinating.

2 Great Cats

The endangered Sumatran tiger has been successfully bred at the National Zoo. Estimates put the population of these dark, striped beauties *(below)* at less than 500 in the wild and 240 in zoos.

3 Asian Elephants

An impressive enclosure featuring an "Elephant Trail", recreates the elephants' natural habitat, allowing them to exercise, forage and live as they would in the wild.

4 Bird House and outdoor flight cage

Here, numerous species of birds display their spectacular colors and elegant motions. The flight cage is a netted structure *(above)* that gives even birds of prey enough headroom to show off.

5 Invertebrate Exhibit

From leaf-cutter ants to a giant Pacific octopus, dozens of fascinating invertebrate species are represented. Visitors can watch scheduled feedings and informal demonstrations.

National Zoological Park Plan

6 Cheetah Conservation Station

Cheetahs and zebras (separated by a fence) display natural behaviors in a grassland setting shared with gazelles and other African savanna-dwellers.

8 Asia Trail

Home to seven Asian species: sloth bears, clouded leopards, fishing cats, red pandas, a Japanese giant salamander, small-clawed otters, and giant pandas.

10 Great Apes

Western lowland gorillas *(below)* are among our closest relatives, sharing about 98 percent of our genes. Their deliberate movements and human-like manner mesmerize observers. The primates are outdoors in the mornings and mid-afternoons.

7 Amazonia

This exhibit recreates the tropical habitat of the Amazon basin and features a variety of animals, including poison arrow frogs *(above)*, titi monkeys, and a two-toed sloth.

9 Reptile Discovery Center

The center's 70 reptile and amphibian species include snakes, turtles, frogs, and the Komodo dragon *(below)*, a venomous Indonesian lizard that can grow as large as 200 lbs (90 kg) and 10 ft (3 m) long.

Zoo Horticulture

The zoo is a lush park for human visitors and its animal residents. Satisfying both presents challenges for the zoo's horticulturists. In the Amazonia exhibit, for example, living avocado and cocoa trees help to re-create the tropical environment of this diverse river basin, while a cheetah wanders around a re-creation of the grasslands of its native African habitat.

The Cleveland Park Metro stop is most convenient for the Connecticut Avenue entrance, avoiding an uphill walk

Arlington National Cemetery

Some of America's most cherished burial sites are found in the 624 acres of the nation's best-known military cemetery. The rolling lawns filled with white tombstones, the Tomb of the Unknowns, and the grave of John F. Kennedy are conspicuous symbols of sacrifices made for freedom. The flags fly at half-staff from before the first and after the last of 25–30 funerals per day, as the graves of veterans continue to multiply. Nearly four million people visit the cemetery every year, some attracted by the historical importance of the site, many wishing to honor those who have died in the nation's wars, others taking part in the funeral of a friend or family member. The cemetery visitors' center provides maps, personalized information, and guidance.

Arlington House

Covering the cemetery on foot requires walking long distances. The most convenient way to get to the cemetery is to take the Tourmobile from any of its 25 stops *(see p117)*. They offer a cemetery-only tour that provides transportation through the cemetery along with commentary and interpretation.

- *Arlington, VA*
- *Map K6*
- *703-607-8000*
- *www.arlingtoncemetery.org*
- *Open Apr–Sep: 8am–7pm daily; Oct–Mar: 8am–5pm daily*
- *Free*
- *Dis. access*

Top 10 Features

1. Lawns of Graves
2. Tomb of the Unknowns
3. Memorial Amphitheater
4. Arlington House
5. Confederate Memorial
6. Grave of John F. Kennedy
7. Tomb of Pierre L'Enfant
8. Seabees Memorial
9. Shuttle Memorials
10. Rough Riders Memorial

1 Lawns of Graves

Approximately 350,000 people are buried on these grounds, marked by unadorned graves, arranged in regular grids, spread across the lawns *(right)*. Although only a small percentage of America's war dead lie here, the expanse gives a tangible picture of the human cost of war.

2 Tomb of the Unknowns

This solemn monument *(right)* is guarded 24 hours a day by The Old Guard. Unknown soldiers of World Wars I and II and the Korean War are entombed here. A Vietnam soldier was interred here, but he was later identified.

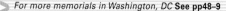

3 Memorial Amphitheater

The setting for the Memorial Day and Veterans Day ceremonies *(see p65)*.

4 Arlington House

This impressive mansion was conceived as a memorial to George Washington, built by his adopted grandson.

For more memorials in Washington, DC **See pp48–9**

5 Confederate Memorial

Although the cemetery is popularly thought to be only for Union soldiers, 482 Confederate soldiers are buried here as well, in circular rows around a central memorial *(above)*.

7 Tomb of Pierre L'Enfant

Honoring the designer of the city grid of Washington *(see p36)*, L'Enfant's monument *(below)* shows the plan of the city within a circle.

Plan of Arlington National Cemetery

9 Shuttle Memorials

This memorial honors the astronauts who died in the explosion of the space shuttle *Challenger* in 1986. A memorial to the 2003 *Columbia* space shuttle tragedy is nearby.

10 Rough Riders Memorial

This dark granite memorial displays the insignia of the First US Volunteer Cavalry (the "Rough Riders") and the battles they took part in during the Spanish-American War.

Civil War Origins

Robert E Lee lived in Arlington House until 1861 when tensions between the Union and the southern states reached a crisis. When Virginia joined the Confederacy and seceded from the Union, Lee became a general of Virginia's military forces. Union troops then crossed the Potomac and took possession of Arlington House. In 1864, Arlington National Cemetery was established to cope with the mass deaths of the Civil War.

6 Grave of John F. Kennedy

The eternal flame *(above)* was lit by Jacqueline Kennedy on the day of the assassinated president's funeral. In 1994 she was buried beside him.

8 Seabees Memorial

A bronze construction worker pauses to make friends with a young child *(below)*. The Seabees – so called from the initials of their name, the Construction Battalion (CB) – performed daring feats in building the military bases needed to win World War II.

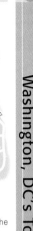

Top 10 Mount Vernon

This graceful mansion, on the banks of the Potomac River, is the second most visited historic residence in America after the White House. George Washington inherited the estate aged 22, and lived at Mount Vernon for over 40 years. With many of the buildings and activities brought back to life, no other place better portrays the character of the first US president, or the role of slavery-based agriculture in the young republic. Be sure to visit the Ford Orientation Center and the Donald W. Reynolds Museum and Education Center for exhibitions and artifacts.

Façade

Costumed events and re-enactments are held throughout the year. See website for details.

The Mount Vernon shops sell seeds of some of the estate's heritage plants.

Outside the main entrance is a complex with a full-service restaurant, the Mount Vernon Inn, offering specialties such as peanut and chestnut soup and salmon corncakes, and an efficient food court, serving snacks.

- *3200 Mount Vernon Parkway*
- *703-780-2000*
- *www.mountvernon.org*
- *Open Apr–Aug: 8am–5pm daily; Mar, Sep, Oct: 9am–5pm daily; Nov–Feb: 9am–4pm daily*
- *Dis. access*
- *Adm $15 adults; $14 senior citizens; $7 children 6–11 years; free under 6 yrs*

Top 10 Features

1. Mansion's Exterior
2. Large Dining Room
3. Front Parlor
4. Little Parlor
5. Study
6. Kitchen
7. Lafayette Bedroom
8. Nellie Custis Room
9. Master Bedroom
10. Cupola

1 Mansion's Exterior

The huge portico that overlooks the Potomac was the president's own design. The house is built from pine, but the exterior was "rusticated" with a decorative treatment that re-creates the look of stone.

2 Large Dining Room

This impressive two-story room *(above)* is formal enough for state business yet is inviting to all. Washington used boards placed on trestles for a table – easier to clear for dancing.

3 Front Parlor

This charming room *(above)* was Washington's favorite place. A copy of the earliest known portrait of Washington, by Charles Willson Peale, hangs here.

4 Little Parlor

Many visitors find this room a highlight of the mansion because it reflects the family life lived in the house. The original harpsichord Washington purchased for his step-granddaughter, Nellie Custis, is displayed.

5 Study

This study *(below)* was the setting for Washington's commercial, political, and public work. French sculptor Jean-Antoine Houdon came to Mount Vernon in 1785 to make a plaster cast of the general's head. The resulting bust is on display in the Donald W. Reynolds Museum on the estate.

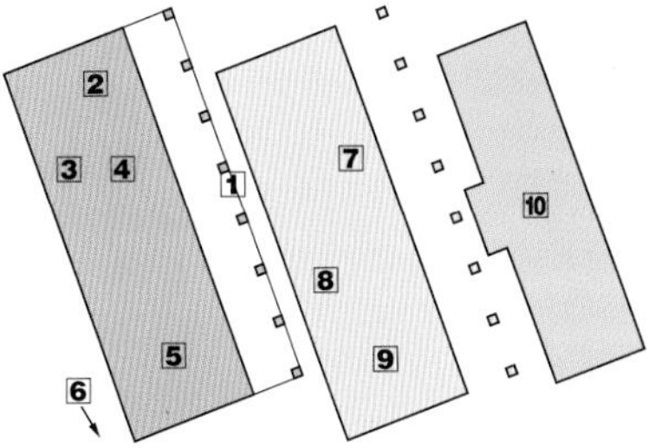

Key

- First Floor
- Second Floor
- Third Floor

9 Master Bedroom

Often called Mrs. Washington's Room *(below)*, this is where George and Martha slept. Mrs. Washington ordered the bed in the 1790s.

6 Kitchen

Mrs Washington directed a staff of slaves in the kitchen *(below)*, and at least two cooks' names have survived, Nathan and Lucy. Much physical labor was required for cooking – fuel and water had to be hauled in by hand.

7 Lafayette Bedroom

This guest bedroom, with its beautiful view of the Potomac, is one of five in the house and is where the Marquis de Lafayette, one of Washington's military aides and a lifelong friend, stayed when visiting.

10 Cupola

The cupola, with its "dove-of-peace" weather-vane, provides light to the third floor and aids air circulation in summer.

Building Mount Vernon

The estate that was to be Mount Vernon had been in the Washington family since 1674. George Washington inherited the estate in 1754 and in the succeeding years built up the property. Additions to the house were underway at the beginning of the Revolutionary War, but the dining room was completed after the war.

8 Nelly Custis Room

Martha Washington's granddaughter, Nelly Custis, lived at Mount Vernon from early childhood. This comfortable room was hers; she even stayed here for a short while after she had married.

Left **16-Sided Treading Barn** Right **Shipping and Receiving Dock**

Top 10 Features of Mr. Washington's Farm

1 16-Sided Treading Barn

With this unique design, George Washington created one of the most aesthetically pleasing and yet efficient working barns. The circular floorplan of the building with its slatted upper floor allowed horses to tread over grain placed on the floor to break the heads from the stalks. The grain then fell through the slats into temporary storage below. The building seen today is a painstaking reconstruction of the original based on thorough research by numerous archeologists and curators.

2 Shipping and Receiving Dock

The wharf of the plantation was the main transportation center for shipping outbound produce and receiving farming and household supplies. The Potomac River was a major carrier of passengers and trade goods in Washington's day. At this evocative spot on its banks, it is easy to imagine the bustle and excitement of early commerce on the river.

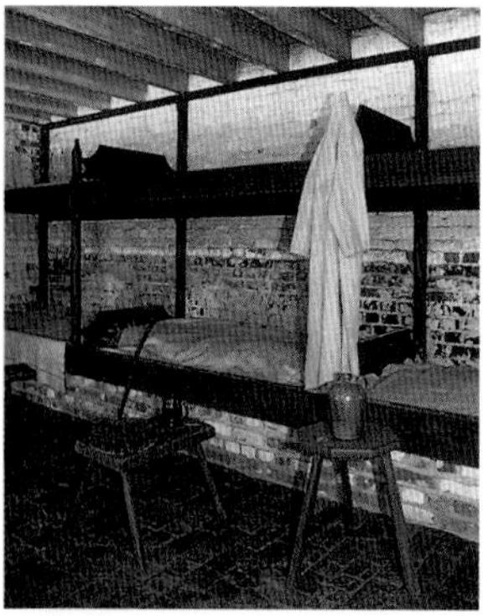

Slave Quarters

Upper Garden

3 River Tours

Visitors can still use the Potomac River to reach Mount Vernon. Two tour boat lines serve the wharf from the city: Spirit Cruise Line and Potomac Riverboat Company. Spirit Cruise Line also offers lovely summer river sightseeing tours originating and ending at Mount Vernon's wharf. *Spirit Cruise Line: 1-866-302-2469, www.spiritofwashington.com • Potomac Riverboat Company: 703-548-9000, www.potomacriverboatco.com*

4 Slave Quarters

Many slaves had living spaces distributed over the plantation so that they were convenient to the work they were assigned. The remaining slaves lived communally in these quarters on the edge of the estate. In his will, Washington freed all his slaves and made provision for their ongoing support. Memorials to his slaves, erected in 1983, are located at the slave burial ground southwest of Washington's tomb, which itself is at the southwest end of the plantation.

5 Upper and Lower Gardens

The wonderfully colorful upper flower garden is densely planted with varieties known to be cultivated in Washington's time. The lower garden is surrounded by boxwood bushes that were planted before Washington's death. This orderly and expansive plot yielded a wealth of vegetables and berries for the plantation.

6 Crop Experimentation

The extremely handsome greenhouse complex was one place where Washington carried out his extensive experimentation with different plant varieties. He always sought to find potentially profitable new crops for his five farms. Slaves were assigned to tend the wood fires to keep the greenhouse warm in the winter.

7 Livestock

Younger visitors to Mount Vernon love the chance to come face-to-face with some of the animals typical of colonial farming, including Ossabaur Island hogs, Hog Island sheep, Bronze Gobbler turkeys, Dominique chickens, Milking Devon cattle, mules, oxen, and horses.

8 New Farming Tools

Washington adapted or invented many new farm implements to suit his various agricultural needs. He designed a new shape for a plow, made improvements to a seeding machine with a barrel feeder, and invented a turnip planter.

Pioneer farming methods

9 Crop Rotation and Soil Conservation

The president was possibly the first farmer to successfully combat the depletion of farming soils. He drew up a chart of his fields and devised planting schedules that would give each field time to be replenished before new crop production began again. He also pioneered the use of organic matter, such as dung and even fish heads, to improve the soil's fertility.

10 Gristmill and Distillery

Located 3 miles (5 km) from Mount Vernon on Route 235, South is Washington's 18th-century water mill, which played an important part in his vision for America as a "granary to the world." Colonial millers grind wheat into flour and corn into meal just as was done in the 1700s. Archaeologists excavated the site of Washington's 1797 whiskey distillery. A fully reconstructed distillery provides demonstrations and hands- on activities. *Gristmill and Distillery open Apr 1–Oct 31: 10am–5pm daily; Adm*

Left **The British burn Washington, 1814** Right **New Deal workers, 1930s**

TOP 10 Moments in History

1 Foundation of the Federal City

The US Constitution, ratified in 1788, provided for "a District (not exceeding ten Miles square) as may, by Cession of Particular States..., become the Seat of the Government of the United States."

George Washington

2 Layout and Design

In 1790 George Washington selected Pierre Charles L'Enfant, a French engineer, to lay out the city. The plan was influenced by Versailles and the city of Paris.

3 War of 1812

The United States declared war on Britain in 1812, seeking freedom of marine trade and the security of US seamen. In 1814 British troops entered the capital and burned government buildings, including the White House and the Capitol. If it had not rained, the whole city might have burned.

4 Expansion

Thomas Jefferson began western expansion by organizing the Lewis and Clark expedition in 1803. The C&O Canal and the Baltimore and Ohio Railroad provided commerce through the mountains and a period of prosperity. New states were added to the Union, and bitter divisions arose connected to the issue of slavery.

5 Civil War

Conflict between the Union and the seceding southern states began on April 12, 1861, and plunged Washington and the nation into crisis. Union supporters, joined by thousands of blacks escaping slavery in the South, doubled the city's population in four years. Although threatened, the city was never taken by Confederate troops, and when the war ended in 1865, Washington was unharmed.

Civil War victory parade

6 McMillan Plan

The McMillan Plan of 1901, named for its congressional supporter, Senator James McMillan, was the first application of city planning in the US. It created much of the layout of the Mall and President's Park seen today.

For historic homes and buildings in Washington, DC **See pp44–5**

7 New Deal

The Roosevelt era (1933–1945) brought tremendous growth to the city. Efforts to bring the nation out of the Great Depression increased the size and number of government agencies, and provided direct funds for construction. Most of the buildings in the Federal Triangle, the completion of the Supreme Court, and the National Gallery of Art were New Deal works.

8 World War II

More than 10 percent of the US population of approximately 115 million was in uniform at the peak of the war, and the central management of these troops remained in Washington.

March on Washington

9 March on Washington

On August 28, 1963, African-American leaders led 250,000 people to rally in front of the Lincoln Memorial in support of equal rights. Dr. Martin Luther King, Jr.'s eloquence in expressing his dream for America, along with the size of the march, gave strong impetus to the struggle for justice for all races.

10 Home Rule

The federal government's policy of maintaining full control over the city was modified with the Home Rule Charter in 1973. This legislation gave the city the power to elect its own mayor, city council, and school board.

Top 10 Citizen Rights of the Constitution

1 Inherent Rights
Freedom of religion, speech, the press, assembly, and seeking redress of citizen grievances.

2 Legality of Arms
The right of the people to keep and bear arms.

3 Quartering of Soldiers
Freedom from housing soldiers in private homes in peacetime and in war, except as prescribed by law.

4 Unjustified Searches
Freedom from unreasonable search and seizure of people, houses, and effects without a warrant.

5 Limits on Prosecutors
A grand jury indictment is required before trial; a person cannot be tried more than once for the same crime; a person cannot be forced to testify against himself; a person's property cannot be confiscated without compensation.

6 Protection of the Accused
Accused persons will be given a trial by a jury of peers, be informed of the charges, be able to confront witnesses, and be represented by counsel.

7 Civil Case Jury Trial
In common law, parties have a right to a trial by jury.

8 Unjust Punishment
The government cannot require excessive bail, impose excessive fines, or use cruel or unusual punishment.

9 Limited Scope
The stated rights do not limit other rights.

10 State Powers
All powers not granted to the US government belong to the states.

Left **James Madison** Right **Funeral of John F. Kennedy**

TOP 10 US Presidents

George Washington

1 George Washington

The United States' first president George Washington (1789–97) was never greater than when he refused to interpret the position of president as equivalent to "king."

2 John Adams

Adams (1797–1801) was among the young nation's most experienced diplomats, having managed affairs in Europe. He was the first US vice president, under Washington.

3 Thomas Jefferson

Jefferson (1801–09) is remembered for his embrace of democracy and his opposition to federal power.

4 James Madison

Madison (1809–17) demurred when he was called "the Father of the Constitution," stating that many minds had contributed, but there is little doubt that the Federalist Papers, which he co-authored, helped gain its ratification.

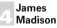

Abraham Lincoln

5 Andrew Jackson

The success of Jackson (1829–37) as a leader in the Battle of New Orleans in 1814–15 made him a national hero. His popularity helped him win battles with Congress and with private business interests over issues such as banking and tariffs.

6 Abraham Lincoln

Unquestionably one of the greatest ever political leaders in any nation, Lincoln (1861–5) overcame inexpressible odds in preserving the Union and beginning the process of freeing slaves.

7 Theodore Roosevelt

The dawning of the 20th century brought an energetic and activist president to the helm. Roosevelt (1901–09) became famous for his military exploits in the Spanish-American war, but is best known for his opposition to business monopolies and pursuing a strong foreign policy. He also established the national parks system in the US.

8 Woodrow Wilson

Wilson (1913–21) was a quiet academic who faced the greatest foreign task the nation had seen – participation in World War I. Wilson successfully promoted a legislative program that controlled unfair business practices, reduced tariffs, forbade child labor, and improved the banking system.

Franklin D. Roosevelt

9 Franklin D. Roosevelt

Roosevelt's (1933–45) efforts to overcome the Great Depression never succeeded in the broadest sense, but they inculcated the federal government with a respect for the rights and needs of the common man and the poorest of the poor. He led valiantly during World War II.

10 John F. Kennedy

Kennedy (1961–3) brought an unprecedented style and flair to the presidency and can be credited with possibly the most important action of the 20th century – the prevention of nuclear war over Soviet missiles placed in Cuba. His assassination cut short his pursuit of a plan for progressive social programs, including more freedom and justice for African-Americans.

Top 10 First Ladies

1 Martha Washington

Martha established the role of the First Lady imitated by her successors. She was famous for accompanying George on military campaigns.

2 Dolley Madison

Dolley's social appeal helped her slightly awkward husband tremendously.

3 Sarah Polk

The wife of James K. Polk (1845–9) was a strong force in the administration, writing speeches for the president.

4 Mary Todd Lincoln

Mary's pleasure at being First Lady was marred by the Civil War and her husband's assassination in 1865.

5 Caroline Harrison

The wife of Benjamin Harrison (1889–93) founded the Daughters of the American Revolution *(see p93)*.

6 Grace Coolidge

The wife of Calvin Coolidge (1923–9) had a charm and tact that made her one of America's best-loved women.

7 Eleanor Roosevelt

Eleanor's interests were equal rights and social justice. She greatly increased the diplomatic role of the First Lady.

8 Jacqueline Kennedy

A stylish socialite, Jackie was an instant hit with the public and visiting diplomats.

9 Hillary Clinton

First lady (1993–2001), senator (2001–2009), and presidential candidate in 2008, she is now President Barack Obama's Secretary of State.

10 Michelle Obama

A Harvard Law School graduate, she worked at the University of Chicago from 1996.

Left **Corcoran Gallery of Art** Center **Freer Gallery of Art** Right **Hirshhorn Museum**

TOP 10 Art Galleries

1 National Gallery of Art

Displaying one of the most distinguished art collections in the world, this gallery gives visitors a broad but in-depth look at the development of American and European art over the centuries *(see pp20–23)*.

2 The Phillips Collection

Opened in 1921, The Phillips Collection is America's first museum of modern art. It is celebrated for its Impressionist works, including Renoir's *Luncheon of the Boating Party*, Pierre Bonnard's *Open Window*, and Degas' *Dancers at the Barre*. *1600 21st St, NW • Map M2 • 202-387-2151 • Open 10am–5pm Tue–Sat (to 8:30pm Thu); 11am–6pm Sun • Adm • Dis. access*

3 Corcoran Gallery of Art

Corcoran exhibitions tilt toward contemporary media, especially photography. The city's first art museum, and one of the three oldest in the United States, is also housed in one of America's most significant Beaux Arts buildings, designed by Ernest Flagg and completed in 1897 *(see p91)*.

Renwick Gallery

4 Hirshhorn Museum and Sculpture Garden

The Hirshhorn exhibits the most varied modern and contemporary art in Washington, DC: its Directions gallery is known for displaying the newest – and sometimes the most controversial – work in the city. The lower level features a selection of recent additions to the collection, while large temporary shows are housed on the second floor, along with modern European sculpture. The third floor displays innovative paintings and sculptures up to the present day *(see p77)*.

5 Renwick Gallery

Many Washingtonians name this gallery as their favorite, not least because it is located in a gorgeous French Renaissance-style building, as well as staging well-organized shows of American crafts. It's also refreshingly quiet in comparison to many other museums and galleries. The second-floor Grand Salon, which has been renovated in the style of a 19th-century picture gallery, displays paintings and sculpture and is decorated with period furniture. Permanent and touring exhibitions of fine craftwork fill other parts of the building *(see p91)*.

6 Freer Gallery of Art

The amazing Peacock Room is among the finest and most subtle examples of interior design found anywhere in the city. Created for a London home by James McNeill Whistler, and recreated here, the elegantly painted walls and ceiling served as a complement to a collection of blue-and-white porcelain. The Freer's 19 galleries host art from Asia, and American art influenced by the Far East. *Jefferson Drive at 12th St SW • Map P5 • 202-633-1000 • Open 10am–5:30pm daily; Closed Dec 25 • Free • Dis. access • www.asia.si.edu*

7 National Museum of African Art

This harmonious building brings architectural features common in Africa to one of the Smithsonian's most innovative museums, built principally underground. The wonderful permanent collection provides the best introduction to the role of art in African culture that one could hope to find *(see p82)*. The pieces on display include ceramics, musical instruments, textiles, tools, masks, and figurines.

8 Arthur M. Sackler Gallery

Another of the underground museums of the Smithsonian, the Sackler is a leading center for the study and display of ancient and contemporary Asian art. Its events bring Asian art and philosophies to life, and its occasional presentations of Tibetan monks carrying out the ritual of sand painting a *mandala* are always huge hits. *1050 Independence Ave SW • Map Q5 • 202-633-1000 • Open 10am–5:30pm daily; Closed Dec 25 • Free • Dis. access • www.asia.si.edu*

9 National Museum of Women in the Arts

This is the only museum in the world dedicated exclusively to displaying the work of women artists, from the Renaissance to the present day. Fascinating and provocative exhibitions explore the work and social role of female artists over the centuries, as well as that of women in general *(see p88)*.

10 Kreeger Museum

This relatively unknown museum houses Impressionist works by 19th- and 20th-century painters and sculptors such as Rodin, Kandinsky, and Monet, as well as a collection of traditional works from Africa and Asia. *2401 Foxhall Rd, NW • Map G5 • 202-337-3050 • Open 10am–4pm Sat; Tours 10:30am and 1:30pm Tue–Fri by appt only • Adm • Dis. access (main level and terrace)*

Indian figurine, Freer Gallery of Art

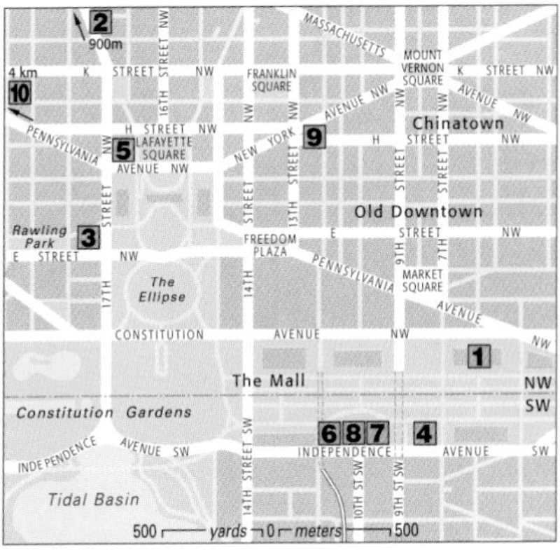

Left **National Air and Space Museum** Right **Dumbarton Oaks**

Top 10 Museums

1 National Air and Space Museum

The 20th century's love affair with flight, from its intrepid beginnings to the mastery of space travel, is explored in this wonderful museum *(see pp16–17)*.

2 National Museum of American History

Mixing the "America's Attic" approach with fine contemporary interpretive exhibits, the museum offers a fascinating look at America's past *(see pp18–19)*.

3 National Museum of Natural History

Must-see exhibits abound here: the Dinosaur Hall with its 87-ft (27-m) *Diplodocus longus*; skeletal remains; the Hope diamond; the Insect Zoo; O. Orkin IMAX® theater *(see p78)*; and a stunning mammal exhibit.

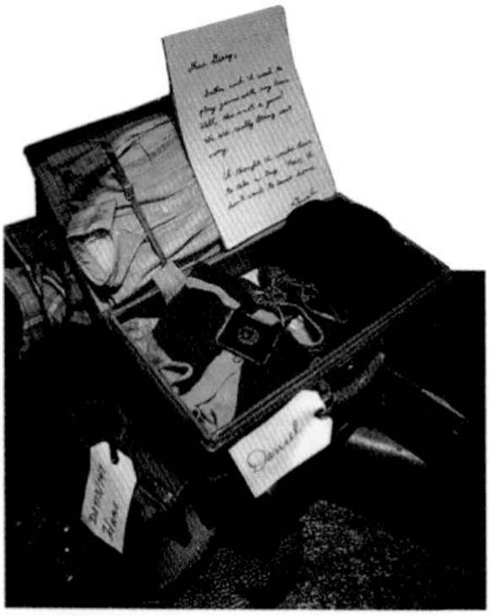

Personal artifacts, United States Holocaust Memorial Museum

Dinosaur Hall, National Museum of Natural History

4 National Museum of the American Indian

The Smithsonian's huge collection of material and artifacts related to Native American art, history, culture, and language moved into its first permanent home in Washington in 2004. Items include North American carvings, quilled hides, feathered bonnets, pottery, and contemporary prints and paintings, as well as objects from Mexico, the Caribbean, and Central and South America *(see p82)*.

5 United States Holocaust Memorial Museum

This ingeniously symbolic building houses documents depicting the Holocaust in Europe before and during World War II, grimly detailing the surveillance and the loss of individual rights faced by Jews, political objectors, gypsies, homosexuals, and the handicapped. Moving eyewitness accounts, photographs, and artifacts tell the story, from "Nazi Assault," to "Last Chapter" *(see p78)*.

6 National Postal Museum

Mail and fun don't naturally go together, but at this wonderfully conceived museum, they do. The little Pony Express saddlebags, the tunnel-like construction representing the desolate roads faced by the earliest mail carriers, and the mail-sorting railroad car entertain and inform visitors *(see p73)*.

7 International Spy Museum

This fascinating museum explores the role that spies have played in world events throughout history. The exhibitions tell the stories of individuals, reveal their missions and techniques, and display their equipment *(see p54)*.

Bill of Rights, National Archives

8 National Archives

The Rotunda of the National Archives proudly displays the foundation documents of American independence and government: the Declaration of Independence, the Constitution of the United States, and the Bill of Rights. The museum features exciting interactive activities in the Public Vaults *(see p82)*.

9 Newseum

This museum boasts an incredible collection of media coverage of events over the past five centuries. Significant moments in history such as the fall of the Berlin Wall and the spine-chilling 9/11 terrorist attacks have their own galleries *(see p87)*.

10 Textile Museum

Founded in 1925, the Textile Museum is one of the world's foremost specialized museums. It holds over 17,000 objects, spanning 5,000 years, and one of the finest collections of Pre-Columbian, Peruvian, Islamic, and Coptic textiles and Oriental carpets. *2320 S St, NW • Map Q4 • Open 10am–5pm Tue–Sat, 1–5pm Sun • 202-667-0441 • Adm*

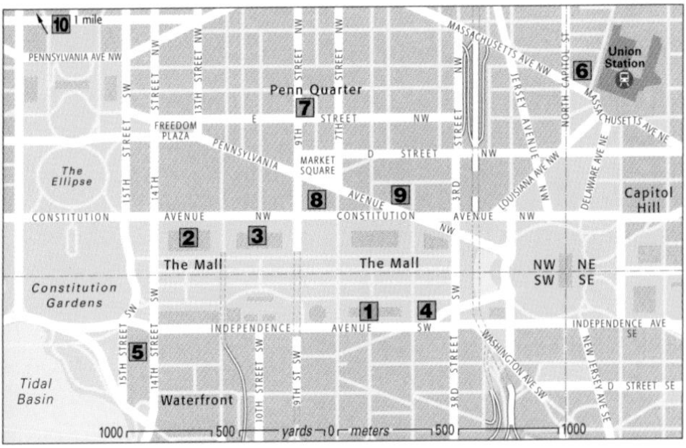

Left **Woodrow Wilson House** Right **Cedar Hill**

Historic Homes and Buildings

1 Ford's Theater

The theater where Lincoln was shot in 1865, has been restored by the federal government. It is now a memorial to the music- and theater-loving president *(see p87)*.

2 Decatur House

Stephen Decatur, a renowned naval hero, built this Federal-style townhouse in 1818. It now houses the White House Historical Association, but has been preserved to evoke the feel of 19th-century middle-class America. *1610 H Street NW • Map N3 • 202-218-4338 • Open 10am–5pm Fri–Sat, noon–3:30pm Sun • Tours: Fri & Sun • Adm*

3 Gadsby's Tavern Museum

George Washington was a patron of this former tavern. The older of the two colonial buildings, dating from 1770, was a growing concern six years before the Declaration of Independence. The second building, the 1792 City Hotel, serves food typical of the 18th century. *134 N Royal St, Alexandria, VA • Map D5 • 703-746-4262 • Open Apr–Oct: 10am–5pm Tue–Sat, 1–5pm Sun–Mon; Nov–Mar: 11am–4pm Wed–Sat, 1–4pm Sun • Adm*

Ford's Theater

4 Carnegie Library

Andrew Carnegie's campaign to build libraries across America (he funded 1,679 in all) changed the country forever. This magnificent Beaux Arts building has been fully restored and is run by the Historical Society of Washington, D.C. *Mt Vernon Sq NW • Map Q3*

5 Woodrow Wilson House

The 28th president was exhausted and demoralized when he left office in 1921, but this Georgian Revival house must have done much to restore his spirits. It now gives a delightful insight into 1920s American life. *2340 S St NW • Map M1 • 202-387-4062 • Open 10am–4pm Tue–Sun • Adm*

6 Cedar Hill

Frederick Douglass and his wife Anna were the first African-American family in Anacostia when they moved here in 1877. Born a slave, Douglass became America's most effective anti-slavery speaker *(see p46)*. Accessible by Tourmobile *(see p117)*. *1411 W St SE • Map E4 • 202-426-5961 • Open Apr 16–Oct 15: 9am–5pm daily (until 4:30pm Oct 16–Apr 15) • Closed Thksgiving, Dec 25, Jan 1 • Dis. access • Adm*

Mary McLeod Bethune Council House

7 Mary McLeod Bethune Council House

The renowned teacher *(see p46)* and advocate for women's and African-Americans' rights bought this Victorian townhouse – now a National Historic Site – in 1935. It is still furnished with her possessions. ⓢ *1318 Vermont Ave NW • Map P2 • 202-673-2402 • Open 9am–5pm Mon–Sat • Free*

8 Old Stone House

The oldest surviving structure in DC, this evocative little building holds demonstrations of crafts and skills of pre-Revolutionary life, such as sheep-shearing, and cooking on an open hearth *(see p100)*.

9 Anderson House

This astounding Beaux Arts mansion from 1905 is decorated in the eccentric style of its original resident, Ambassador Larz Anderson. Its 600-ft (180-m) long ballroom is spectacular. ⓢ *2118 Massachusetts Ave NW • Map M2 • Open 1–4pm Tue–Sat • Free*

10 Sewell-Belmont House

The 1800 construction date makes this enchanting home one of the oldest on Capitol Hill, and a National Historic Landmark. It is now a museum of women's emancipation *(see p72)*.

Top 10 Architectural Sights

1 National Building Museum

In this cavernous interior, displays examine architecture, engineering, design, and city planning *(see p87)*.

2 Eisenhower Executive Office Building

The extravagant decoration is a favorite with architecture buffs *(see p91)*.

3 Treasury Building

This Greek Revival building maintains features from its 1836 beginnings *(see p92)*.

4 The Octagon

This odd-shaped building is now a museum of architecture and design *(see p92)*.

5 Library of Congress

The most extensive library ever built contains exquisite decoration *(see pp24–5)*.

6 Old Post Office Pavilion

A Romanesque revival skyscraper completed in 1899 now contains shops and a food court *(see p57)*.

7 Pope-Leighey House

The city's most innovative Frank Lloyd Wright design. ⓢ *Alexandria, VA • US 1 and Rte 235*

8 Supreme Court

This marble edifice never fails to delight *(see p71)*.

9 Gunston Hall

George Mason's refurbished house is luminescent with vivid colors and designs. ⓢ *Mason Neck, VA • Rte 242, south of US 1*

10 Cox's Row

Outstanding examples of domestic architecture of the early 19th century. ⓢ *3327–29 N St NW • Map K2 • Closed to the public*

Left **Lincoln Memorial** Right **Mary McLeod Bethune Council House**

TOP 10 Places of African-American History

1 Lincoln Memorial

This memorial touches the hearts of all African-Americans because of Lincoln's steadfastness in ending slavery in the US. It was here that Martin Luther King, Jr. made his "I Have a Dream" speech *(see p48)*.

2 Metropolitan African Methodist Episcopal Church

This church was important in sheltering runaway slaves before the Civil War, and its pulpit has hosted many respected speakers, including Frederick Douglass, Martin Luther King, Jr., and Jesse Jackson. *1518 M St, NW • Map P3*

3 Anacostia Museum and Center for African-American History and Culture

This museum explores the role that African-Americans have played in the culture of the nation. Temporary exhibitions examine specific events or survey the work of important black artists.
1901 Fort Place, SE • Map E4 • Open 10am–5pm daily • Dis. access • Free

4 Cedar Hill

Frederick Douglass, a former slave, made many speeches for the rights of African-Americans, and was an adviser to Abraham Lincoln. He and his wife, Anna, moved into this Gothic-Italian-style house in 1877. In the garden is a humble stone hut nicknamed "The Growlery," which Douglass used as a study *(see p44)*.

5 Mary McLeod Bethune Council House

A former cotton-picker, Bethune rose to be a leading educator of African-Americans and an activist for equal rights. Her house was the headquarters of the National Council of Negro Women, which she founded. During the Franklin D. Roosevelt administration, she was a valued adviser *(see p45)*.

6 Supreme Court

In one of its most notable decisions, the Supreme Court aided African-Americans' quest for equality in the 1954 Brown v. Board of Education trial, in which the "separate but equal" system of education was overturned. It was a turnaround from the 1896 Plessy v. Ferguson decision that supported segregation *(see p71)*.

7 Mount Zion United Methodist Church

Believed to be the first black congregation in the District, founded in 1816, Mount Zion's original building was an important stop on the Underground

"The Growlery," Cedar Hill

For more moments in history in Washington, DC **See pp36–7**

Supreme Court

Railroad. Its present red-brick site was built in 1884. Behind the church is a small cottage containing a collection of artifacts reflecting the black history of Georgetown. ✆ *1334 29th St • Map L2 • 202-234-0148 • Open by appt*

8 Lincoln Park

This pleasant urban park does justice to its dedication to Abraham Lincoln. The 1974 Robert Berks statue of Mary McLeod Bethune shows the great educator passing the tools of culture on to younger generations. The Emancipation Statue by Thomas Ball (1876) shows Lincoln holding his Proclamation in the presence of a slave escaping his chains *(see p74)*.

9 Frederick Douglass Museum

Another site associated with the statesman and abolitionist, this was Douglass's home for nearly 10 years from the mid-1870s. Artifacts associated with Douglass are displayed here *(see p74)*.

10 Benjamin Banneker Park

This waterfront park is named in honor of a renowned 18th-century free black mathematician and astronomer. ✆ *10th and G Sts, SE • Map Q6*

Top 10 African-American Figures

1 Ralph Bunche
The first African-American to receive the Nobel Peace Prize, because of his diplomatic efforts in the UN.

2 Duke Ellington
The musical genius was a native Washingtonian. He played his first paid performance on U Street.

3 Hiram Rhodes Revel
The first African-American to take a seat as US senator, representing Mississippi.

4 Paul Lawrence Dunbar
Dunbar rose from poverty to gain recognition as a poet – the first African-American to do so – publishing his first collection in 1892.

5 Harriet Tubman
The best-known figure who freed slaves through the Underground Railroad.

6 Ida B. Wells-Barnett
This celebrated crusader against anti-black government actions also marched in the 1913 women's suffrage rally.

7 Marian Anderson
In 1939 the singer was barred from Constitution Hall because of her race, so gave her Easter Sunday concert at the Lincoln Memorial instead.

8 Eleanor Holmes Norton
Norton has been effective as the District's non-voting House member, lobbying to promote Washington issues.

9 Walter E. Washington
Mayor of Washington from 1974–8, the first elected mayor in the city for over 100 years.

10 Barack Obama
In November 2008, Obama was elected as the U.S.'s first African-American president.

Left **Jefferson Memorial** Center **Franklin D Roosevelt Memorial** Right **US Navy Memorial**

Memorials and Monuments

1 Lincoln Memorial

The majestic monument to the president who preserved America's unity and began the long process of ending slavery is built in the form of a Greek temple. Daniel Chester French designed the enormous statue of a seated Abraham Lincoln in 1915, and it is among America's most inspiring sites, especially for its association with African-Americans' struggle for equality and opportunity *(see p78)*.

2 Washington Monument

This spire is the dominant feature on the city skyline, 555 ft (170 m) high and gleaming in its marble cladding. One of the tallest freestanding masonry constructions in the world, built between 1848 and 1884, it can be seen from miles around the city *(see p78)*.

3 Jefferson Memorial

One of Jefferson's favorite Classical designs, the Pantheon in Rome, inspired this graceful monument. Dedicated in 1943 on the 200th anniversary of Jefferson's birth, it houses a 19-ft (6-m) bronze statue of the president by Rudolph Evans. It is especially enchanting when floodlit at night *(see p82)*.

4 Franklin Delano Roosevelt Memorial

This popular memorial has four outdoor rooms, representing Roosevelt's four terms as president. Each is a composition of statues, water, plants, and engraved quotations of the president. The memorial is a focus for activists for disabled citizens – Roosevelt was partially paralyzed by polio *(see p82)*.

5 Vietnam Veterans' Memorial

This simple structure – a V-shaped black granite wall on which are carved the names of those who died in this divisive war – has moved millions of visitors. The memorial, built in 1982, is the work of Maya Lin, at the time a 21-year-old architecture student at Yale *(see p79)*.

6 Korean War Veterans Memorial

Nineteen exhausted foot soldiers plod forward, determined on their goal. These 7-ft (2-m) steel statues are the dominant element in a memorial to the Americans who died in the UN's "police action" in Korea. A wall is etched with faces of actual soldiers. A circular pool invites quiet reflection *(see p82)*.

Lincoln Memorial

Iwo Jima Statue (Marine Corps Memorial)

7 Iwo Jima Statue (Marine Corps Memorial)

Marines struggling to erect the Stars and Stripes on a ridge at Iwo Jima serves as a memorial to all marines who have fought for their country. The Pacific island saw fierce fighting, resulting in 7,000 American deaths, during World War II. *1400 N Meade St, Arlington, VA • 703-289-2500 • Map K5 • Free • Dis. access*

8 World War II Memorial

This 7.5-acre memorial, built to honor US veteran soldiers and civilians of World War II, includes commemorative columns, a Freedom Wall, landscaping, and fountains. *National Mall • Map N5 • Free • Dis. access*

9 African-American Civil War Memorial

"The Spirit of Freedom," a 1996 sculpture by Ed Hamilton, depicts African-American Union soldiers facing the enemy. *1000 U St NW • Map P1 • Free • Dis. access*

10 US Navy Memorial

The fountains that surround this plaza contain recirculated water from all the seven seas. Flagstaffs suggest the rigging of a tall ship *(see p88)*.

Top 10 Statues

1 Abraham Lincoln
The marble vision dominates Lincoln's memorial.

2 Neptune Fountain
Roland Hinton Perry created this grouping at the Library of Congress *(see p25)*.

3 Albert Einstein
This 1979 bronze by Robert Berks shows the great thinker in front of the National Academy of Sciences. *2101 Constitution Ave NW • Map M4*

4 Benjamin Franklin
Jacques Jouvenal's statue at the Old Post Office honors Franklin's creation of the US Postal Service. *1100 Pennsylvania Ave NW • Map P4*

5 First Division Monument
A shining tribute to the First Infantry Division of World War I. *State Place & 17th St NW • Map N4*

6 Andrew Jackson
This heroic equestrian statue was created by Clark Mills in 1853. *Lafayette Sq NW • Map N3*

7 Winston Churchill
A 1966 sculpture by William M McVey symbolizes the friendship between Britain and the US *(see p54)*.

8 Grant Memorial
This magnificent grouping took Henry Merwin Shrady 20 years to complete *(see p74)*.

9 Theodore Roosevelt
Paul Manship's work shows the president gesticulating to his listeners. *Roosevelt Island • Map L4*

10 Joan of Arc
This 1922 work was a gift from the women of France to the women of the US. *Meridian Hill Park, Florida Ave & 16th St NW • Map P1*

Left **Theodore Roosevelt Island** Right **US Botanic Garden**

Top 10 Green Spaces

1 US Botanic Garden

The gleaming glass-walled conservatory building is a beautiful home for this "living plant museum." Microclimates, such as desert, oasis, and jungle, reveal the variety and beauty of plant adaptations. Don't miss the primitive ferns and other plants dating back 150 million years. Outside is the variegated National Garden with an environmental learning center *(see p72)*.

2 Enid A. Haupt Garden

This "rooftop" garden is inspired by the culture on display beneath it in the Smithsonian Museums. The Island Garden beside the Sackler Gallery reflects the Asian world, with its moon gate, pools, and cherry and beech trees. The Fountain Garden, next to the Museum of African Art, sets a Moorish tone, with cascading waters and shaded seats.

10th St & Independence Ave, NW • Map P5 • Open Memorial Day–Sep 30: 6:30am– 8pm daily; Oct–Memorial Day: 7am– 5:45pm daily • Free • Dis. access

3 Dumbarton Oaks

Magnificent trees, including ancient oaks, soar above the park and gardens surrounding this historic Federal-style house. Designed by Beatrix Jones Farrand, the gardens range from formal to more casual settings. From March to October they are ablaze with wisteria, roses, lilies, perennial borders, and chrysanthemums. Pools and fountains tie the verdant ensemble together *(see p99)*.

4 National Arboretum

A world-acclaimed bonsai display – some of the bantam trees are almost 400 years old – is one of the many collections that flourish season to season on these 446 acres dedicated to research, preservation, and education. Azaleas, dogwoods, holly, magnolias, herbs, roses, and boxwoods abound. A stand of columns, formerly on the US Capitol, adds a classical air.

3501 New York Ave, NE • Map E3 • Open 8am–5pm daily • Free • Dis. access

US Botanic Garden

5 Rock Creek Park

This vast national park meanders with its namesake creek, offering something for everyone: woodland trails, 30 picnic areas, 25 tennis courts, a golf course, playing fields, and nature programs for kids and adults *(see p53)*.

For outdoor activities in Washington, DC **See pp60–61**

Chinese Pavilion, National Arboretum

6 C&O Canal

Canalboats on this 184-mile (295-km) waterway, dating back to the early 19th century, carried cargo between Maryland and Georgetown for 100 years before the railroad put it out of business. The canal is now a National Historical Park, a haven for walkers and cyclists along its towpath and for canoeists and boaters in its waters. Catch a mule-drawn boat ride at Georgetown or Great Falls *(see p99)*.

7 Theodore Roosevelt Island

This wooded island on the Potomac River is the perfect memorial to the president remembered as a conservationist. A 17-ft (5-m) statue of Teddy Roosevelt is the centerpiece of what otherwise is a monument to nature – a space for birdwatching, hiking, and fishing. *George Washington Memorial Parkway • Map L4 • Open 6am–10pm daily • Free • Dis. access*

8 Bartholdi Park and Fountain

The French sculptor of the Statue of Liberty, Frédéric Auguste Bartholdi (1834–1904), also created this reflection of *belle époque* majesty. The 30-ft (9-m) sculpture's three caryatids support a circular basin surmounted by three tritons. A small garden surrounds the fountain like the setting for a gemstone *(see p72)*.

9 Kenilworth Park and Aquatic Gardens

The 14-acre (6-ha) Aquatic Gardens began as a hobby for W.B. Shaw in 1882, then became a commercial water garden, where many varieties of water lilies were developed. Now a national park, the gardens are home to water lilies and lotuses, plus many varieties of birds, frogs, turtles, and butterflies. Adjacent Kenilworth Park features acres of recreational areas and meadows. *Gardens: 1550 Anacostia Ave, NE; Map E3; Open 7am–4pm daily; Free; Dis. access • Park: Kenilworth & Burroughs Aves; Map E3; Open 8am–dusk daily, closed Thanksgiving, Dec 25, Jan 1; Free; Dis. access*

10 Glover Archbold Trail

From Van Ness Street to the Potomac River, this 3-mile (5-km) trail in the northwest of the city passes beneath beautiful old trees that host an abundance of birds, in keeping with its designation as a bird sanctuary in 1924. The trail joins the C&O Canal towpath, and other routes. *South of Tenleytown Metro station on Wisconsin Ave, then left on Van Ness St, NW*

Pierce Mill, Rock Creek Park

Left **National Air and Space Museum** Right **National Building Museum**

Children's Attractions

1 National Air and Space Museum

Kids' dreams are founded on and inspired by these ravishing soaring devices and spectacular rockets, while their parents and grandparents can reminisce over the early days of aviation and see how far we've come. Children can experience a full-motion flight in an aircraft simulator *(see pp16–17)*.

2 National Zoological Park

The animals in Washington, D.C.'s zoo are housed in large, recreated natural habitats and are close enough to be clearly observed. Sea lion demonstrations never fail to delight. The Kids' Farm is an educational, interactive, outdoor exhibit, where children can touch and learn about farmyard animals *(see pp28–9)*.

3 National Geographic Museum

These first-class exhibits explore the major domains of society, including foreign cultures, nature, archaeology, and superb photography. The museum is at the forefront of designing and constructing interactive and immersive displays to involve visitors in their fascinating subject matter. There is a rolling program of changing exhibitions, as well as permanent collections, which reflect the diversity of the ever-changing world in which we live. The well-stocked shop complements the exhibitions.
17th & M Sts NW • Map N2 • Open 9am–5pm Mon–Sat, 10am–5pm Sun • Closed Dec 25 • Dis. access • Free

National Zoological Park

4 Verizon Sports Center

Children love the energetic events here. Among the acts that perform here are touring ice skating spectaculars, professional wrestling, hockey games and many top-name pop and rock acts. The food is better than usual at this arena and, naturally, is geared toward kids *(see p87)*.

5 National Building Museum

This interesting museum runs regular programs for families, where children and parents can learn about various methods of construction, architecture, and design. Together, families can build edible houses, learn about different construction materials, or solve a city's transport problem The permanent and visiting exhibitions will also appeal *(see p87)*.

6 National Aquarium

Turtle, National Aquarium

The star attraction for children here is the 2pm feedings and aquarist talks: sharks on Mondays, Wednesdays, and Saturdays; piranha on Tuesdays, Thursdays, and Sundays; and alligators on Fridays. The aquarium houses about 300 specimens in its glass tanks and provides easy-to-understand informative material about freshwater habitats and the oceans and the marine life they support. The staff are extremely friendly and helpful, and children's questions are handled with aplomb *(see p88)*.

7 National Museum of American History

This kid-friendly museum has some great hands-on action for its younger visitors, including the Spark Lab where interactive exhibits are designed to explore the process of invention. Activities are targeted at children aged six to twelve, but there is also the "under-5 zone" for younger children. The award-winning "Invention at Play" exhibition uses games and experiments to look at similarities between the way children and adults play, and the creative processes used by inventors *(see p18)*.

8 National Museum of Natural History

There is plenty here for young visitors, in particular the Insect Zoo featuring live specimens of giant hissing cockroaches and large leaf-cutter ants, and the Dinosaur Hall which contains a cast of a nest of dinosaur eggs and reconstructions of dinosaur skeletons. The interactive Hall of Mammals features 274 taxidermy exhibits, and the Discovery Room allows children (and adults!) to hold and touch objects such as crocodile heads and elephant tusks. The Live Butterfly Pavilion is home to species from around the world. ✆ *Constitution Ave & 10th St, NW • Map P4 • Open 10am–5:30pm daily • Closed Dec 25 • www.mnh.si.edu • Dis. access • Free*

9 Smithsonian Carousel

Located in front of the Arts and Industries Building at the Smithsonian is a delightful authentic carousel with brilliantly painted hand-carved animals. It only operates in good weather, but don't miss this bit of old-world fun if you have the chance. It also makes a refreshing break for kids beginning to tire of the surrounding museums. ✆ *900 Jefferson Drive SW • Map P5 • Open 10am–5pm daily • Closed Dec 25 • Adm*

10 Rock Creek Park Nature Center

The short nature trail here is only 1 mile (1.5 km) long *(see p51)*, so it is easily negotiated by children. Many native species of animals can be spotted en route, including foxes, racoons and deer. There is also a small planetarium. A number of activities that appeal to children, including arts and crafts workshops, are scheduled throughout the year. On a sunny day, this is also a great place to bring along a picnic lunch and enjoy one of the city's truly natural environments. In other parts of the park, there are also tennis courts and horse-riding trails. ✆ *5200 Glover Rd NW • Map J2 • 202-895-6070 • Open 9am–5pm Wed–Sun • Free*

Left **Washington Post newsroom during the Watergate scandal** Right **Dumbarton Oaks**

TOP 10 Places of Politics and Intrigue

1 Embassy Row

Since the 19th century, Embassy Row, the string of great mansions heading west from Dupont Circle up Massachusetts Avenue, has been a hotbed of gathering and suppressing information. Today, 46 embassies and chanceries here help shape foreign policy by allowing issues to be discussed without the glare of public announcement. *Map M1 & M2*

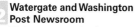

Churchill statue, Embassy Row

2 Watergate and Washington Post Newsroom

The Watergate complex became the most infamous apartment and office complex in the world when a bungled burglary there, as part of an espionage campaign against President Nixon's opponents, led to his resignation *(see p96)*. The newspaper that played the main role in revealing the scandal, the *Washington Post*, offers tours to groups (minimum 10) by request; contact four weeks in advance. *Watergate: Virginia Ave, NW; Map M3 • Washington Post newsroom: 1150 15th St, NW • Map P3 • 202-334-7969*

Watergate complex

3 Katherine Graham House

The Georgetown home of Katherine Graham, publisher of the *Washington Post* from 1963 to 2001, provided a salon for politicians of every persuasion to discuss issues of the day. *2920 R St, NW • Map L2 • Closed to the public*

4 Dumbarton Oaks

In 1944, representatives of China, the Soviet Union, United Kingdom, and the United States developed proposals at Dumbarton Oaks for an international body to bring peace among nations. The result was the United Nations *(see p99)*.

5 International Spy Museum

This fascinating museum examines clandestine operations in political and military decisions. Artifacts include an example of Enigma, the World War II German encryption device, and a camera designed to photograph through walls. *800 F St, NW • Map Q4 • 202-393-7798 • Opening hours are subject to change; Closed Thanksgiving, Dec 25, Jan 1 • Dis. access • Adm*

6 Private Clubs

Lobbyists regularly frequent private clubs in the downtown area, such as the National Democratic Club and Army and Navy Club, as well as country clubs such as the Congressional Country Club, where a little discreet politicking is accepted and expected.

For political scandals in Washington, DC **See p96**

7 House of the Temple Library

Home to the Supreme Council since 1915, the appeal of this library lies in the insights it offers into famous Washingtonians, especially the large display on J. Edgar Hoover. *1733 16th St, NW • Map P2 • Tours 10am–4pm Mon–Thu • 202-232-3579*

House of the Temple Library

8 FedEx Field

The Washington Redskins are something of a local religion *(see p61)*. At home games, the cigar bar, club seating levels, and luxurious suite- and box-seating are filled with lobbyists, campaign donors, and activists schmoozing with each other.

9 Political Dining

The Monocle *(see p75)* has a history of fostering alliances and deals – it is the closest restaurant to the Senate side of the Capitol. The Caucus Room *(see p63)* is funded by political insiders, and popular for high-profile power-dining. *The Monocle: 107 D St, NE • Map S4 • 202-546-4488 • $$$$*

10 The Inn at Little Washington

This famed restaurant, west of the city, is a prime spot for entertaining to impress, and the 90-minute drive there and back provides time for lobbyists to bond and bargain – assuming the car is bug-free. *Middle & Main sts, Washington, VA • 540-675-3800 • $$$$$*

Top 10 Congressional Leaders in History

1 James K. Polk
A supporter of Andrew Jackson, Polk (1795–1849) led the fight in the administration's conflict with the banks. He became president in 1845.

2 Daniel Webster
Webster (1782–1852) is credited as the finest speaker in defense of the Union in debates over slavery.

3 Henry Clay
A great orator (1777–1852) known for his proposals for compromise over slavery.

4 William Boyd Allison
Allison (1829–1908) was a major force in shaping US laws passed in the 19th century.

5 Henry Cabot Lodge
This distinguished patrician (1850–1924) opposed corrupt influences of big business.

6 George W. Norris
Norris (1861–1944) was author of the 20th Amendment to the US Constitution, clarifying issues related to tenure in office.

7 Joseph Taylor Robinson
The death of this leader (1872–1937) was attributed to overwork associated with New Deal proposals *(see p37)*.

8 Margaret Chase Smith
Smith (1897–1995) publicly condemned the anti-Communist smear tactics of Senator Joseph McCarthy.

9 Sam T. Rayburn
Rayburn (1882–1961) witnessed the administrations of eight presidents.

10 John W. McCormack
McCormack (1891–1980) was instrumental in passing the Civil Rights Acts of 1964 and 1968.

Left **Neiman Marcus, Friendship Heights** Right **Georgetown shops**

Top 10 Shopping Areas

1 The Fashion Centre at Pentagon City

The local cliché is that this expansive mall has become the main downtown shopping area, even though it is not in the city center. But it is less than 10 minutes away by Metro, and there is a train stop right in the mall. Nordstrom and Macy's are the anchors here, but there are over 170 other establishments, including Abercrombie & Fitch, Banana Republic, and Joseph A. Banks. A food court, spa, and restaurants complete the attractions. *1100 S Hayes St • Map C4 • Dis. access*

2 Shops at Georgetown Park

This wonderfully restored building – a former stable, power generation plant, and repair shop for streetcars – is worth seeing in itself. It is extraordinarily airy and quiet for a mall. There are high-quality fashions, art, home furnishings, jewelry, and kitchenware. The food court is small but pleasant. *3222 M St, NW • Map L3 • Dis. access*

3 Friendship Heights

This area in the far northwest of the city is home to some of the most elegant and exclusive retail outlets in the city. Mazza Gallerie is a small, upscale mall at 5300 Wisconsin Ave, NW. Kron Chocolatier *(see p112)* is here, along with Neiman Marcus, Saks Fifth Avenue Men's Store, and Williams-Sonoma Grande Cuisine. Other stores on Wisconsin Avenue include Tiffany & Co (No. 5500), Dior (No. 5471), and Cartier (No.5454). *Map G2*

4 Potomac Mills Mall

This is among the best-known discount outlet malls on the East Coast and one of the largest in the world. Over 200 stores have discounts up to 70 percent off suggested retail prices. Their own in-mall TV station broadcasts special deals and newly available products. A shuttle bus runs from a number of stops in the metropolitan area. *2700 Potomac Mills Circle 307, Woodbridge, VA • Dis. access*

5 The Shops at National Place

This mall is worth a visit even for nonshoppers. The architecture in the four-story space is inspired, and there are quiet areas to have a coffee. The shops are mainly boutiques and small emporiums. *529 14th St or 1331 Pennsylvania Ave, NW • Map P4 • Dis. access*

National Place

For tips on shopping in Washington, DC **See p120**

Old Post Office Pavilion

6 Tysons Corner Center and Galleria at Tysons II

This huge shopping complex has many anchor stores – Nordstrom, Bloomingdale's, Lord & Taylor, Saks Fifth Avenue, Macy's, and Neiman Marcus. Two separate malls are separated by Chain Bridge Road. There's plenty of parking, and some hotels run shuttle buses. ✎ *Tysons Corner Center: 1961 Chain Bridge Rd, McLean, VA • Galleria at Tysons II: 2001 International Drive, McLean, VA; Dis. access*

7 Watergate Mall

This small shopping area includes St-Laurent Rive Gauche, Valentino, and Saks Jandel. The wares are expensive, but fashion-seekers can sometimes find a sales bargain. ✎ *2650 Virginia Ave, NW • Map M3 • Dis. access*

8 Georgetown

Probably the most famous shopping area in the city, partly because of the hundreds of shops but also for the pervasive sense of style. Fashion shops are especially numerous, but antiques, art, books, records, electronics, wine, and other products are found here. The main area is between K and T and 27th and 38th streets, NW, especially on Wisconsin Avenue, NW, and M Street, NW. ✎ *Map L2*

9 Old Post Office Pavilion

Centrally located in Washington's first skyscraper, this small downtown indoor mall has a number of boutiques and eateries. Plans are underway to convert the site into a luxury hotel. ✎ *1100 Pennsylvania Ave, NW • Map P4 • Dis. access • www.oldpostofficedc.com*

10 Eastern Market

The market is an appetizing source of picnic provisions on weekdays and a carnival of arts and crafts vendors on weekends. The big Eastern Market Flea Market is across 7th Street, SE, on Saturdays, and a busy, colorful and vibrant Arts and Crafts Market spills into neighboring streets on Saturdays and Sundays. Several shops – notably a vintage clothing store and an antiques dealer – and a number of cafés are located on the same block. On the west side, between the market and Pennsylvania Avenue, SE, are shops selling toys and children's items, books, art and prints, and goods from Asia and South America *(see p74)*.

Eastern Market

Left **National Theatre** Right **Warner Theater**

TOP 10 Theaters

1 Ford's Theater

The tragedy of Lincoln's assassination here in 1865 kept this theater closed for over 100 years, but now it is the home of a vibrant theater company as well as being a museum, center for learning, and historic landmark *(see p87)*.

2 Arena Stage

Internationally renowned as a pioneering non-profit theater for over five decades, Arena has produced plenty of high-quality drama. The Arena reopened at Mead Center for American Theater in late 2010, making it the leading center for production, development, and study of American theater. *1101 6th St SW • Map Q6 • 202-488-3300*

Auditorium, Ford's Theater

3 Shakespeare Theatre

Top actors, directors, designers, and lighting experts are involved in every dazzling production here. Although specializing in Shakespeare, the company also mounts works by other playwrights *(see p71)*. *450 7th St NW • Map Q4*

4 National Theatre

A wonderful venue for touring shows, the National Theatre opened in 1835. Since then every US president has attended at least one of its performances. Many Broadway hits have staged their premiere here, including *Showboat* and *West Side Story*. *1321 Pennsylvania Ave NW • Map P4 • 202-628-6161*

5 Kennedy Center

From Shakespeare to Sondheim, from gripping drama and opera to light-hearted comedies and musicals, the many theater productions at this landmark arts center are almost always critically acclaimed. There are a variety of performance spaces catering to different styles, seating from just a few hundred people to more than 2,000 *(see p91)*.

6 Woolly Mammoth Theater Company

Widely acknowledged as Washington's most daring theater company, Woolly Mammoth stages new and innovative productions. *641 D St NW • Map Q4 • 202-393-3939*

The Kennedy Center

7 Folger Theater

Visitors get a unique experience in this Elizabethan Theatre, which strongly suggests the setting in which Shakespeare's works were originally performed. Works of the Bard and his near contemporaries are featured, and performances of medieval and baroque music fill the schedule *(see p71)*.

8 Gala Hispanic Theater

The recipient of a huge number of awards, this theater mounts works in Spanish with simultaneous English translation. Brilliant productions of works from the classical to the absurd attract a diverse audience. *3333 14th St NW • Map D3*

9 Studio Theater

Off-Broadway hits, classics, and experimental fare make up the season at this performance landmark. Two theater spaces are available for the engrossing and often splendid productions here. *1501 14th St NW • Map P2*

10 Harman Center for the Arts

The Harman Center is a modern 21st-century performing arts center and an expanded stage for the Shakespeare Theater Company. It offers great theater, ballet, and musical performances. *Harman Hall: 610 F St NW • Map Q4*

Top 10 Entertainment Venues

1 Verizon Center

The home of D.C.'s basketball and hockey teams has many attractions beyond the games *(see p87)*.

2 Warner Theater

You'll find Broadway shows, comedians, and concerts here. *13th & E Sts NW • Map P4*

3 Carter Barron Amphitheater

Open-air stage in Rock Creek Park. Performances throughout summer *(see p64)*. *4850 Colorado Ave NW • Map D2*

4 Coolidge Auditorium

The home of the Library of Congress music series *(see p25)*. *Library of Congress, 10 1st St SE • Map S5*

5 Lisner Auditorium

This university theater features everything from world music to orchestras. *21st and H Sts NW • Map M3*

6 Nationals Park

Home to the Nationals Baseball team, this park is the city's latest highlight. *1500 S Capitol St SE • Map E4*

7 DAR Constitution Hall

The largest concert hall in D.C. *1776 D St NW • Map N4 • Dis. access*

8 Lincoln Theater

An intimate setting for jazz, soul, and gospel music. *1215 U St NW • Map P1*

9 Wolf Trap

An open-air venue for big names in entertainment. *1551 Trap Rd, Vienna, VA • Metro West Falls Church*

10 Nissan Pavilion

Rock stars perform at this open-air arena. *7800 Cellar Door Drive, Bristow, VA • Rte I-66 to exit 44*

Left **In-line skaters** Right **Kayaking**

TOP 10 Outdoor Activities

1 Boating

Thompson Boat Center in Georgetown rents kayaks, rowing shells, canoes, and sailboats to reach Roosevelt Island and tour the waterfront. The Washington Sailing Marina rents sailboats for excursions on the Potomac. Call about certification requirements. *Thompson Boat Center: 2900 Virginia Ave, NW; 202-333-9543; Open Mar–Oct: 6am–8pm Mon–Sat, 7am–7pm Sun • Washington Sailing Marina: 1 Marina Drive, Dangerfield Island, Alexandria, VA; 703-548-9027; Open 9am–6pm daily*

2 In-Line Skating

Rock Creek Park has been named one of the top 10 sites in the nation for in-line skating, but most bike trails allow skaters as well. You can rent skates and protective gear from one of the numerous in-line skating companies in the area. *Map C4*

3 Running

Runners are everywhere in Washington. The Mall is popular, as are the walkways around the Tidal Basin, Georgetown Waterfront, the C&O Canal *(see p99)*, and Rock Creek Park *(see p50)*.

Runners

Cyclists

4 Cycling

Both Thompson Boat Center and the Washington Sailing Marina rent bicycles, and Capital Bikeshare has 150 stations in the city. Favorite routes are the C&O Canal towpath and the Mount Vernon Trail along the George Washington Parkway to Mount Vernon *(see pp32–5)*. Bike and Roll offers tours and rentals. *Bike and Roll: Old Post Office Pavilion, 1100 Pennsylvania Ave, NW; 202-842-2453; www.bikeandroll.com • Capital Bikeshare: www.capitalbikeshare.com • Map P4*

5 Golf

There are over 100 golf courses in the vicinity, the most famous being the Congressional Country Club private course in Bethesda. The East Potomac Park course is public, as is the Rock Creek Park Golf Course. Langston Golf Course was among the first African-American courses in the US. *East Potomac Park: 972 Ohio Drive, SW (Hain's Point); Map D4; 202-554-7660 • Rock Creek Park Golf Course: 6100 16th St, NW; Map J1; 202-882-7332 • Langston Golf Course: 2600 Benning Rd, NE; Map E3; 202-397-8638*

Amateur soccer game

6 Hiking

The 4-mile (7-km) Western Ridge Trail and 5-mile (8-km) Valley Trail, both in Rock Creek Park *(see p50)*, are scenic and gentle. The 11.5-mile (18.5-km) Capital Crescent Trail follows the old B&O Railroad route through Georgetown north to Bethesda. Trail information available at www.trails.com.

7 Informal Team Sports

Volleyball, dodge ball, rugby, softball, team Frisbee, and even polo are played on various fields at the western end of the Mall.

8 Tennis

The East Potomac Park Tennis Center is operated by the National Park Service. Indoor and outdoor courts are available. *East Potomac Park Tennis Center: 1090 Ohio Drive, SW • Map D6 • 202-554-5962*

9 Horseback Riding

The Rock Creek Park Horse Center provides scheduled trail rides and riding lessons for all levels. No experience is necessary for the guided rides, and the center provides the required helmet and other necessary equipment. *Rock Creek Horse Center: 5100 Glover Rd, NW • Map J2 • 202-362-0117 • Open noon–6pm Tue–Fri, 9am–5pm Sat & Sun*

10 Climbing

The city of Rockville has a climbing gym in its Civic Center Park. *860 Avery Lane, Rockville, MD; 240-314-8643, www.rockvillemd.gov/climbinggym*

Top 10 Spectator Sports

1 Washington Redskins

The National Football League Redskins are a year-round obsession. Games are at FedEx Field in Maryland. Season tickets only.

2 Washington Wizards

The National Basketball Association team plays at the Verizon Center *(see p87)*. Buy tickets at the box office.

3 Washington Capitals

The National Hockey League team plays home games at the Verizon Center.

4 DC United

Robert F. Kennedy Memorial Stadium is home to professional soccer. *Robert F. Kennedy Stadium: 2400 E Capitol St, SE • 202-547-9077*

5 Baseball

Major league baseball at Nationals Park in DC, and Camden Yards in Baltimore.

6 Washington Mystics

The women's basketball professional league plays home games at the Verizon Center.

7 Citi Open

This mid-summer tournament attracts major tennis pros. *www.leggmasontennisclassic.com*

8 Georgetown University Basketball

Fast-paced action at the Verizon Center.

9 University of Maryland Athletics

ACC football and national basketball teams lead a varied program. *College Park, MD • 202-397-SEAT*

10 Naval Academy Football

The spectacle at these games is unmatched. Schedule and tickets: www.navysports.com

Left **Madam's Organ** Center **The DC Improv** Right **The Park at Fourteenth**

TOP 10 Nightspots

1 Blues Alley
Marvelous drinks and food in an intimate club setting featuring today's best jazz performers. *1073 Wisconsin Ave, NW • Map L2*

2 Madam's Organ
For years this Adams Morgan fixture has defined the middle-of-the-road club scene in the city. Live music and dancing. Their slogan is "Where the Beautiful People go to get ugly." *2461 18th St, NW • Map D3*

3 The Park at Fourteenth
Dress to impress at this popular downtown stop, which attracts its share of fashionable locals. This elegant four-level club is known for its smooth music and trendy cocktails. *920 14th St, NW • Map P3*

4 9:30 Club
Edgy, creative live music by some of the best national and international bands and performers, in a straight stand-up-and-play atmosphere. The young crowds are boisterous and know their music. *815 V St, NW • Map Q1*

Blues Alley

5 The DC Improv
This local establishment of the chain of comedy clubs books some outstanding talents. There is also a restaurant that serves a full menu. *1140 Connecticut Ave, NW • Map N3*

6 Birchmere
Billing itself as a "music hall," the Birchmere has continually presented top folk, country, blues, bluegrass, and swing bands. Good snacks and a full bar. *3701 Mt Vernon Ave, Alexandria, VA • Map C5*

7 Café Saint-Ex
Sophisticated yet laid-back, Saint-Ex has aviation-themed decor. A DJ plays in the down-stairs bar on most nights. *1847 14th St, NW • Map P1*

8 Marvin
The lower level of this low-key lounge is a restaurant, while the upper level lures the crowds with its lively bar and rooftop garden. *2007 14th St, NW • Map P1*

9 18th Street Lounge
One of DC's most exclusive nightclubs. Despite the dress code and strict doormen, the scene is cool and approachable. *1212 18th St, NW • Map N2*

10 Black Cat
An indie venue with two concert rooms, a pool table, and a juke box, as well as a small café serving vegan and vegetarian meals. *1811 14th St, NW • Map P1*

Left **Citronelle** Center **Kinkead's** Right **Nora**

TOP 10 Restaurants

1 Citronelle
Condé Nast *Traveler* magazine named this one of the 50 most exciting restaurants in the world *(see p105)*.

2 Kinkead's
A power-dining venue, known for its fine seafood dishes. Live jazz on weekends *(see p97)*.

3 Nora
Refined New American cuisine made from organically grown ingredients. ✆ *2132 Florida Ave, NW • Map R2 • $$$$*

4 Acadiana
This elegant restaurant offers modern interpretations of Louisiana dishes by chef Jeff Tunks. ✆ *901 New York Ave, NW • Map Q3 • $$$$*

5 Obelisk
A fixed-price menu of the finest Italian dishes. ✆ *2029 P St, NW • Map N2 • $$$$*

6 West End Bistro
Located in the Ritz-Carlton, this bistro of renowned chef Eric Ripert offers American cuisine. ✆ *1190 22nd St, NW • Map M3 • $$*

7 The Caucus Room
Where legislators meet to hammer out agreements. Classic steak and seafood. ✆ *401 9th St, NW • Map Q4 • $$$$$*

8 CityZen
Eric Ziebold sets the standard for fine dining at this award-winning American restaurant. ✆ *1330 Maryland Ave, SW • Map P5 • $$$$$*

9 Vidalia
Southern charm meets European elegance in this acclaimed restaurant. ✆ *1990 M St, NW • 202-659-1990 • Map N3 • $$$$*

10 1789
Federal-style townhouse serving a medley of lamb, oysters, and other dishes *(see p105)*.

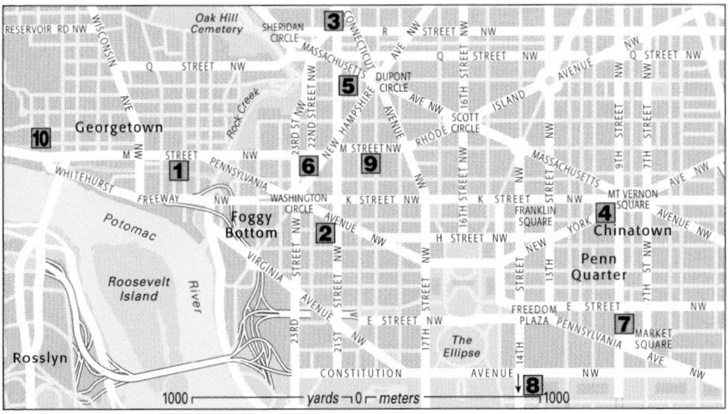

For a guide to restaurant prices **See p75**

Left **Smithsonian Folklife Festival** Right **National Cherry Blossom Festival**

TOP 10 Festivals and Cultural Events

1 Smithsonian Folklife Festival

Fascinating and entertaining cooking, storytelling, craft-making, dancing, music, and art fill the National Mall for two weeks around Independence Day (July 4). One of the largest and best cultural events in the world.

2 National Cherry Blossom Festival

The Tidal Basin is surrounded by beautiful Japanese cherry trees, which originated with 3,000 specimens given to the city in 1912 by the mayor of Tokyo. The festival celebrating their spring bloom includes a parade, performances, and such offbeat events as a sushi-making contest. *Late Mar–mid-April*

3 Shakespeare Free for All

The first two weeks of June bring free performances of works of Shakespeare in the outdoor amphitheater in Rock Creek Park. Presented by the Shakespeare Theater *(see p58)*, the productions are of excellent quality. Free tickets available at several sites.

Smithsonian Folklife Festival

4 Washington Home and Garden Show

At the end of winter, locals and visitors alike are revitalized by the early jolt of spring provided by the riot of colorful flowers and inviting landscapes re-created indoors. The air itself is restorative, scented by the spring blossoms. *Washington Convention Center, 801 Mount Vernon Place, NW (between 7th and 9th Sts) • Map Q3 • Early Mar*

5 National Book Festival

Organized and sponsored by the Library of Congress, this festival takes place over a weekend in September on the National Mall and is free and open to the public. Around 50 authors of fiction, non-fiction, and children's books give readings, presentations, and signings; plus there are giveaways, promotions, and activities sponsored by a number of publishing companies. *www.loc.gov/bookfest*

6 Washington National Cathedral Christmas Services

In early December, the cathedral *(see pp26–7)* inaugurates the Christmas season with an open house featuring bagpipes, group singing, pageantry, and stunning seasonal decorations. Then, throughout the season, music and concerts are presented, culminating with the elaborate celebrations of Christmas Eve and Christmas Day.

Washington Flower and Garden Show

7 Filmfest D.C.

This top-quality and lively film festival has brought the best of world cinema to the city since 1986. The most exciting new films are shown during two weeks in April at various venues, and discussions and film-oriented events are held at theaters, auditoriums, and cafés across the city.

8 Capital Jazz Festival

This annual three-day festival of jazz and blues boasts an impressive line-up of national and international artists and bands. *Merriweather Pavilion, Columbia, MD • www.capitaljazzfest.com • Early Jun*

9 Washington Nationals

Big league baseball returned to Washington in 2005 after a 30-year absence. The Washington Nationals fill the stands of the Nationals Park from April to October. *1500 S Capitol St SE • Map E4 • 888-632-NATS • www.nationals.com*

10 Chinese New Year

Ten days of parades, fireworks, special menus at the restaurants, and unique events in Chinatown. Simply pass through the ornate arch at 7th and H streets, NW. *Late Jan–early Feb*

Top 10 One-Day Events

1 Smithsonian Kite Festival
Competitions include home-built kites, fighting kites, and others. *National Mall • Late Mar–early Apr*

2 Independence Day
The celebration culminates with a fireworks display synchronized with patriotic music. *National Mall • Jul 4*

3 White House Easter Egg Roll
Children's activities, music, and egg rolling. Advance tickets only. *Easter Mon*

4 National Christmas Tree Lighting
The decorations are joyous. *The Ellipse • Early Dec*

5 National Frisbee Festival
The Frisbee dogs always steal the show. *Washington Monument • Late Aug*

6 Memorial Day
Concerts, ceremonies, and a parade along Constitution Avenue honor those who have died serving their country. *Last Mon in May*

7 National Symphony Labor Day Concert
The official end of summer. *US Capitol • Labor Day*

8 International Gold Cup Steeplechase Races
Take place at the peak of fall's colored foliage. *Great Meadows Events Centers, The Plains, VA • Mid-Oct*

9 St Patrick's Day
A parade on Constitution Ave, SE. *Sun before Mar 17*

10 Martin Luther King, Jr. Day
Church services held. Check local papers for details. *3rd Mon in Jan*

For current information about the annual Filmfest, visit their website at www.filmfestdc.org

Left **John Brown's fort, Harper's Ferry** Center **Whiteoak Canyon, Skyline Drive** Right **Baltimore**

Excursions from Washington

1 Annapolis, Maryland

This enticing city on the Chesapeake Bay is one of the great sailing centers on the East Coast as well as being home to the US Naval Academy. It has a bustling business district and numerous historic houses, such as the home of William Paca, the governor who signed the Declaration of Independence. *Rte 50 • William Paca House: 186 Prince George St; Open 10am–5pm Mon–Sat, noon–5pm Sun; Closed Dec–Mar • Adm*

2 Harpers Ferry, West Virginia

Before the Civil War, John Brown carried out his famous raid against government troops here, protesting the legality of slavery in the United States. The picturesque little town around the old Potomac waterfront has been preserved and is filled with exhibits about the history of this important industrial, shipping, and military center. This is a fine place to hike, and picnics on the riverfront are popular. *Rte 340*

3 Skyline Drive, Virginia

This delightful winding road passes 107 miles (170 km) through the mountain and valley scenery of Virginia's Shenandoah National Park. Numerous hiking trails to isolated peaks, waterfalls, and rare forest environments begin from the main highway. *Off Rte I-66*

4 Baltimore, Maryland

Called "Charm City" by its residents and promoters, Baltimore offers museums of art, industry, baseball, science, railroads, and marine trade along with historic sites from every American period. Its phenomenal National Aquarium is among the finest in the world. The historic Lexington Market, established in 1782, is still going strong with over 140 food vendors. *Rte I-95*

5 Chincoteague and Assateague, Virginia

Assateague Island is famed for its wild ponies. The pony swim and auction, held on the last Wednesday and Thursday of July, is a major attraction. The Chincoteague National Wildlife Refuge is a paradise for bird-watchers and nature buffs. The local seafood is first-rate, and the ice cream made here is justifiably famous. *Off Rte 13*

William Paca House, Annapolis

6 Middleburg

In the heart of Virginia hunt country, Middleburg is a captivating little town. Its seasonal farmers market, local horse races, and its antique shops, galleries, and fine restaurants draw visitors from all over. *Rte 50 • Farmers Market: mid-May–mid-Nov: Sat*

The Red Fox Inn, Middleburg

7 Fredericksburg, Virginia

This city on the Rappahannock River offers colonial homes, moving Civil War sites, and a downtown filled with shops and restaurants. A marked walking tour lays out milestones in the city's history. *Rte 1*

8 Frederick, Maryland

Noted for its bridges, Frederick is a city steeped in the memory of 19th-century life and the Civil War. In addition, it has an exceptional artistic and cultural life. *Rte I-270*

9 Manassas Battlefield

This Civil War battlefield is where Confederate and Union soldiers fell by the thousands fighting for conflicting visions of the nation's future. Manassas experienced two pitched battles, the first an opening confrontation of untested troops, the second a bloodbath. Guided tours are available. *Off Rte I-66*

10 Gettysburg, Pennsylvania

The three-day battle of Gettysburg in 1863 was the bloodiest of the Civil War, killing over 51,000. Lincoln's famous address dedicating the cemetery here expressed determination to persevere in maintaining the Union and began to put the great conflict in perspective. The Gettysburg National Military Park is among the most visited sites on the East Coast. *Rte 15*

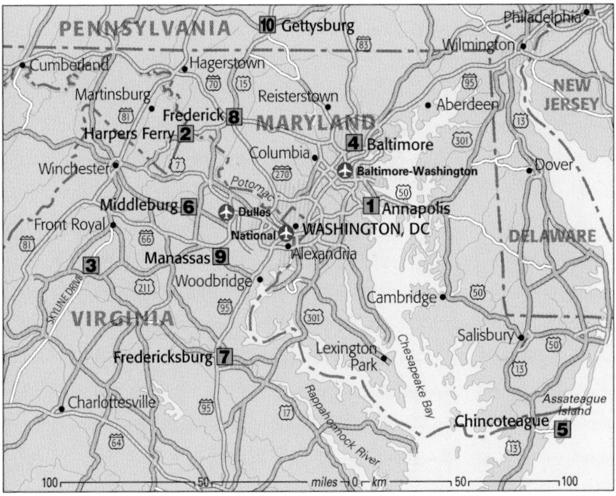

Following pages: **Pennsylvania Avenue**

AROUND TOWN

Left **Library of Congress** Right **Supreme Court Building**

Around Capitol Hill

BUSTLING WITH THE BUSINESS OF GOVERNMENT, *Capitol Hill is also a destination for shopping, entertainment, food and drink, or simply strolling its handsome neighborhood streets. Approached from the west, the area begins with the meticulously landscaped US Capitol complex, which, in addition to the Capitol itself and its giant staff office buildings, includes the splendid US Botanic Garden, the stately Supreme Court Building, and the three buildings of the Library of Congress. Union Station, to the north, is filled with diverse shops and restaurants and is one of the finest railroad terminals in the world. Farther to the east, beyond the Capitol, lies the residential area, containing pleasing East Coast domestic architecture. Eastern Market on 7th St, SE, serves as a community center, and a pleasant walk farther to the east leads to Lincoln Park, with its outstanding memorial statues* (see p74), *beginning at 11th St.*

Statue, Sewall-Belmont House

TOP 10 Sights

1. **US Capitol**
2. **Library of Congress**
3. **Union Station**
4. **Folger Shakespeare Library and Theater**
5. **Supreme Court Building**
6. **US Botanic Garden**
7. **Bartholdi Park and Fountain**
8. **Sewall-Belmont House**
9. **Eastern Market**
10. **National Postal Museum**

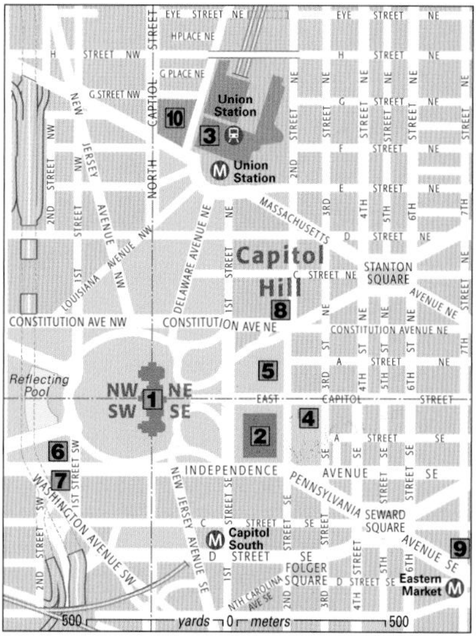

1 US Capitol

Symbolizing both government power and the control of that power by the people, the Capitol crowns the east end of the National Mall *(see pp8–11)*.

2 Library of Congress

The world's largest collection of books, documents, and sound and video recordings is housed in three huge buildings to the east of the Capitol. The architecture of the Jefferson Building makes it a tourist destination in itself *(see pp24–5)*.

3 Union Station

Opened in 1907, this magnificent Beaux Arts building is still a fully functional transportation hub. The lofty barrel-vaulted concourse, decorated with 70 lbs (32 kg) of gleaming gold leaf, is one of the great public spaces in the city – the Washington Monument, laid on its side, would easily fit within its length. Over 23 million people pass through the station each year. A $160 million restoration, completed in 1988, made the terminal an important retail and entertainment center, with over 130 shops, numerous restaurants, and a 9-screen cinema, as well as expanding its transportation role. ✎ *50 Massachusetts Ave, NE • Map R4 • Dis. access*

Union Station

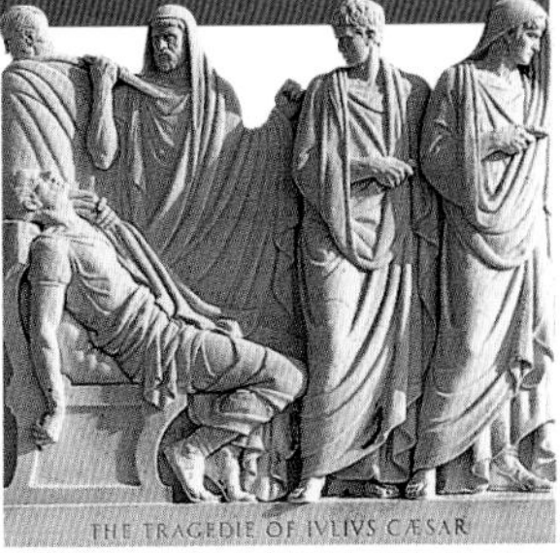

Folger Shakespeare Library and Theater

4 Folger Shakespeare Library and Theater

The Folger has the world's largest library of printed editions of Shakespeare's works, and performances at the 16th-century-style theater give viewers an insight into Shakespeare and his times. There is also a huge supporting collection of Renaissance works in other fields, as well as playbills, musical instruments, and costumes. The elegant Neo-Classical building, a 1929 design by Paul Philippe Cret, is on the National Register of Historic Places *(see p59)*. ✎ *201 East Capitol St, SE • 202-544-4623 • Map S5 • Open 10am–5pm Mon–Sat • Dis. access • Free*

5 Supreme Court Building

The home of the highest seat of the judicial branch of the US government is a handsome Neo-Classical building designed by Cass Gilbert – the architect of the beautiful Woolworth Building in New York City – and completed in 1935. On its west pediment, above the marble columns of the main entrance, is inscribed in bold letters the famous motto "Equal Justice Under Law" *(see p46)*. ✎ *1st St and East Capitol St, NE • 202-479-3211 • Map S4 • Open Mon–Fri 9am–4:30pm except federal holidays • Dis. access • Free*

Capitol Hill Residences

In the early 19th century, the area east of the Capitol was filled with a motley collection of boarding houses and taverns where members of Congress stayed during legislative sessions. During the 19th and into the 20th centuries, a diverse mix of housing styles – Federal townhouses, manor houses, Queen Anne, interspersed with two-story frame dwellings – developed. The protected Capitol Hill Historic District is now the largest historic residential district in the city.

6 US Botanic Garden

Long valued by Capitol Hill residents as a quiet retreat, the Botanic Garden conservatory is home to some 4,000 living plants that have been arranged into themes and biosystems, such as Plant Exploration, Jungle, Oasis, and Medicinal Plants. The wedge-shaped National Garden, situated to the west of the Conservatory, includes glorious colorful outdoor displays. The main court is a wonderfully fragrant spot and a perfect place to sit and rest *(see p50)*. *On the Capitol grounds at Maryland Ave and 1st St, SW • 202-225-8333 • Map R5 • Open 10am–5pm daily • Dis. access • Free*

7 Bartholdi Park and Fountain

Another oasis for Capitol Hill visitors, this immaculate park is bursting with flowers and ornamental plants. Its symmetrical design radiates out from the fine Gilded Age cast-iron Bartholdi Fountain, a three-story high construction of supple human forms, European-style lights, and a non-stop flow of water *(see p51)*. *1st St & Washington Ave, SW • Map R5 • Dis. access • Free*

8 Sewall-Belmont House

Built in 1750 and expanded into its current mansion size in 1800, this house is one of the most historic in Washington. It is thought that one past resident, Albert Gallatin, Treasury Secretary for Jefferson and Monroe, may have worked out the financial details of the Louisiana Purchase – which nearly doubled the size of the United States – here. The house was the only private residence burned during the War of 1812 because only from here did Americans fire on the invading British *(see p36)*. The completely rebuilt home was bought by the National Women's Party in 1929 and remains their home today. Visitors can see the elaborate but homely period furnishings of the house's past, as well as the museum's fascinating collection of objects and documents fundamental to the suffragist and feminist movements in the United States, and the oldest feminist library in the US *(see p45)*. *144 Constitution Ave, NE • 202-546-1210 • Map S4 • Tours noon–4pm Wed–Sun • Donation*

Bartholdi Fountain

Hallway, Sewall-Belmont House

9 Eastern Market

Completed in 1873, Eastern Market has been a key element in Capitol Hill's history. Designed by a prominent local architect, Adolph Cluss, the market symbolized the urbanization of the city at the end of the Civil War. Since then, it has served as a meeting place for residents, and as a focal point in the revitalization of the area. It has been repeatedly threatened with closure, however, the south hall has reopened following a fire in 2007 *(see p74)*.

10 National Postal Museum

The US Postal Service delivers over 600 million items of mail every day, and this ingenious museum manages to communicate the human scale of the system. Exhibits explore the history of mail from pre-Revolutionary America to modern technological developments. The philatelic collection is one of the largest in the world *(see p42)*.

2 Massachusetts Ave, NE • Map R4 • www.postalmuseum.si.edu • Open 10am–5:30pm daily • Dis. access • Free

A Day Around Eastern Market

Morning

Before a day of shopping, begin with a bit of history at the **Library of Congress** *(see pp24–5)*, a handsome example of the Italian Renaissance style, with unsurpassed interiors. The first tour is at 10:30am.

Turn right to East Capitol Street, right again, and continue one block to the **Folger Shakespeare Library and Theater** *(see p71)*. The Elizabethan theater is enchanting, and the material displayed is both rare and fascinating.

Walk east to 7th Street and turn right. A little over two blocks farther on is **Eastern Market** *(see p74)*. On weekends it is surrounded by arts and crafts vendors and flower stalls. **The Market Lunch** *(see p75)* inside is a great choice for lunch.

Afternoon

If you visit the market on a Saturday, spend the afternoon at the Capitol Hill Flea Market, across the street from Eastern Market. It features 100 or more vendors selling antiques, Oriental rugs, fabrics, fine art photographs, jewelry, and other items. If the flea market is closed, walk a block south of Eastern Market and visit Woven History and Silk Road *(311–5 7th St, SE • Map S5 • 202-543-1705 • Open 10am–6pm daily)* for its fabrics, rugs, and crafts from Asia and South America.

To return home, turn right and the Eastern Market metro stop is straight ahead of you.

Left **Ebenezer United Methodist Church** Right **Ulysses S. Grant Memorial**

TOP 10 Best of the Rest

1 Eastern Market
Weekends are the time to visit to take in the crafts and farm produce stalls *(see p57)*. *7th St & C Street, SE • Map S5*

2 Ebenezer United Methodist Church
The first congregation of African-American Methodists and Episcopals in Washington. It also became home to the first public school for black children after the Emancipation Proclamation. *420 D St, SE • Map S5 • Open 10am– 2pm Mon–Fri • Free*

3 Ulysses S. Grant Memorial
This equestrian grouping honors the Union victory in the Civil War. Sculptor Henry Shrady (1871–1922) took 20 years to complete the work *(see p49)*. *US Capitol • Map R5*

4 Emancipation Monument
Lincoln holds the Emancipation Proclamation while the last slave, Archer Alexander, breaks his chains *(see p47)*. *Lincoln Park • Metro Eastern Market*

5 Statue of Mary McLeod Bethune
This modern sculpture of the great African-American educator and activist symbolizes knowledge handed down through generations *(see p47)*. *Lincoln Park • Metro Eastern Market*

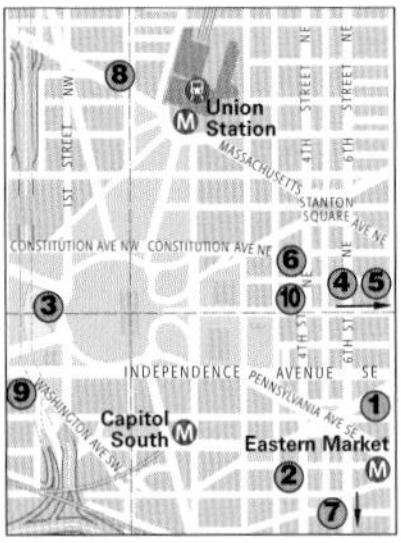

6 Frederick Douglass Museum
The home of the African-American activist contains many of his possessions, including a document proclaiming him a "freed man" *(see p47)*. *320 A St, NE • Map S4 • Open 9am–4pm daily, by appt. only • 202-544-6130 • Free*

7 Christ Church
This elegant church, built in 1805, had many prominent parishioners, including presidents Madison and Monroe. *620 G St, SE • Map S6*

8 National Guard Memorial Museum
This gallery remembers citizens who gave their lives to protect the nation. *1 Massachusetts Ave, NW • Map R4 • 202-408-5887 • Open 10am–4pm Mon–Fri • Dis. access*

9 Voice of America
Most of VOA's programming, broadcasting US news around the world, is created at these studios. *330 Independence Ave, SW • Map R5 • 202-203-4990 for tours • www.voatour.com*

10 Alleys and Carriageways
The alleys of Capitol Hill, notorious in the 19th century for their squalid and cramped residences, have today been turned into charming little homes. *Map S5*

Price Categories

For a three-course meal for one with half a bottle of wine (or equivalent meal), taxes and extra charges.		
	$	under $30
	$$	$30–$50
	$$$	$50–$75
	$$$$	$75–$100
	$$$$$	over $100

Left **Johnny's Half Shell** Right **The Monocle**

TOP 10 Places to Eat

1 Dubliner Pub
An Irish pub with free-flowing pints and good hearty food. Try the lamb with mustard crust or the shepherd's pie. There is Irish music from 9pm and an outdoor patio in summer. *4 F Street • Map R4 • 202-737-3773 • Dis. access • $*

2 The Market Lunch
This lunchtime counter with nearby tables serves barbecue food North Carolina style, with a specialty in seafood. Try the crabcakes and oyster sandwiches. Saturday breakfast is very popular. No alcohol. *Eastern Market, 225 7th St • Map S5 • 202-547-8444 • No credit cards • Dis. access • $*

3 The Monocle
The Monocle claims to be the first fine-dining restaurant on Capitol Hill. A favorite with the Kennedys, it still holds a place of honor among the power-dining crowd and is known for its delicious fresh steaks and seafood. *107 D St, NE • Map S4 • 202-546-4488 • $$$$*

4 Café Berlin
A German restaurant in a townhouse setting. *Wiener schnitzel*, pork loin with sauerkraut, and other hearty dishes. The desserts are tempting. *322 Massachusetts Ave, NE • Map S4 • 202-543-7656 • Dis. access • $$*

5 Bullfeathers
Popular with politicians, this bar has a good selection of salads, sandwiches, and hamburgers. Crowded at weekday lunchtimes. *410 1st St, SE • Map R5 • 202-448-2701 • Closed Sun • Dis. access • $$*

6 Johnny's Half Shell
An interesting menu – fresh kumamotos, gumbo, oysters, tequila-cured gravlax, and more. *400 N Capitol St, NW • Map R4 • 202-737-0400 • Dis. access • $$$*

7 Le Pain Quotidien
Fresh bread and pastries baked daily. Great sandwiches, salads, soups, and desserts. *660 Pennsylvania Ave, SE • Map S5 • 202-459-9148 • Dis. access • $*

8 Capitol City Brewing Company
Stylish bar serving tasty food and great beers. *2 Massachusetts Ave, NE • 202-842-2337 • Map R3 • $$$*

9 Tortilla Coast
Great Tex-Mex food. George W. Bush was a customer before he was elected president. *400 1st St, SE • Map R5 • 202-546-6768 • Dis. access • $*

10 Sonoma
California cuisine, cheese platters, and an eclectic menu of wines. *223 Pennsylvania Ave, SE • Map S5 • 202-544-8088 • $$$*

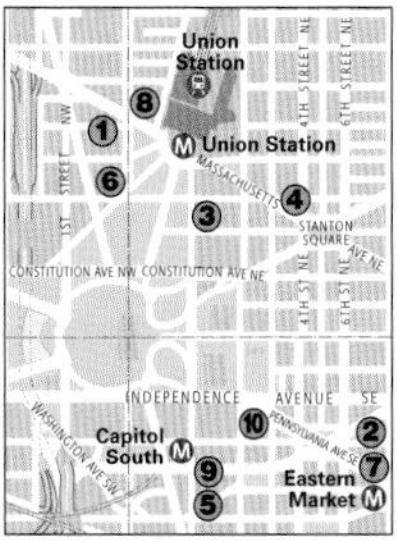

Note: *Unless otherwise stated, all restaurants accept credit cards and serve vegetarian meals*

Left **National Museum of American History** Right **United States Holocaust Memorial Museum**

The Mall and Federal Triangle

EVEN WASHINGTONIANS WHOSE DAILY PURSUITS *rarely take them to the Mall regard this magnificent open expanse as the heart of the city. A grassy park with carefully preserved trees, the Mall stretches 2.5 miles (4 km) from the Capitol to the east to the Potomac River, just beyond the Lincoln Memorial, to the west. Alongside and nearby are the core symbols of the city and the nation: memorials to past suffering and triumphs, the workplaces of the federal government, and the Smithsonian Institution museums, entrusted with "the increase and diffusion of knowledge." The Mall also serves as a national public square – it fills to capacity for the dazzling Fourth of July celebration and fireworks display, while the Smithsonian Folklife Festival* (see p64) *brings food, dance, storytelling, and crafts from all over the world. And the space is enlivened daily with ordinary people jogging, strolling, or just enjoying the extraordinary views.*

Museum of Natural History

Top 10 Sights

1. **National Museum of the American Indian**
2. **National Gallery of Art**
3. **National Air and Space Museum**
4. **National Museum of American History**
5. **Hirshhorn Museum and Sculpture Garden**
6. **National Museum of Natural History**
7. **United States Holocaust Memorial Museum**
8. **Washington Monument**
9. **Lincoln Memorial**
10. **Vietnam Veterans' Memorial**

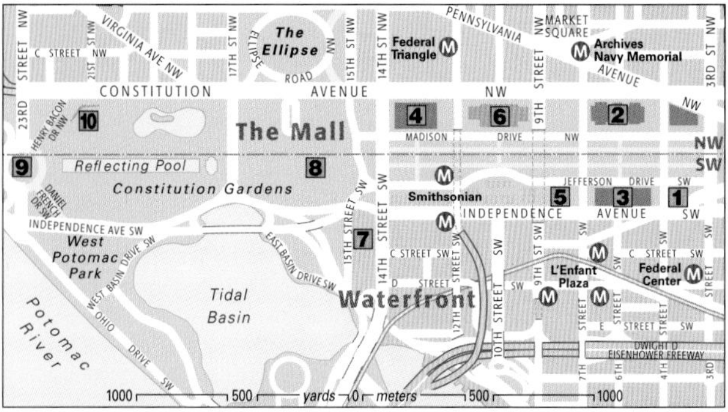

1 National Museum of the American Indian

This fascinating museum enshrines 10,000 years of Native American life and culture, and acknowledges the contributions native peoples have made to the history of the Americas. The collection includes over 800,000 items, 7,000 of which are on display. Exhibits include pre-Columbian gold figurines, beadwork, textiles, and pottery from the Arctic to Patagonia. The building itself has been designed in harmony with Native American cultural beliefs. The entrance faces east to meet the morning sun, and light spills in reflecting the importance of the sun within Amerindian culture *(see p42)*.

2 National Gallery of Art

Stroll through this building surrounded by illustrious artworks dating from before the Renaissance to the current day. The sculpture garden is a hit for its outdoor setting, summer jazz concerts, a winter ice-skating rink, and café *(see pp20–23)*.

3 National Air and Space Museum

The story of flight, one of the most stirring in human history, is dramatically depicted in this favorite museum, renowned for its collection of precious artifacts of the challenging experience of flying *(see pp16–17)*.

Central Plaza, Hirshhorn Museum

National Museum of American History

4 National Museum of American History

The story of the United States of America, from its beginnings to the present day, is told here through public icons and examinations of the daily lives of ordinary people. The many permanent exhibits include Julia Childs' TV kitchen, the John Bull Locomotive, and the Star-Spangled Banner Gallery. "America on the Move" draws on the museum's unparalleled collections and looks at all the modes of transportation from 1876 to the present *(see pp18–19)*.

5 Hirshhorn Museum and Sculpture Garden

The only public gallery in the city with the sole focus on modern and up-and-coming art, this museum's holdings and exhibitions of contemporary international works are exceptional. The unusual circular building, designed by Gordon Bunshaft and completed in 1974, provides a striking setting for outdoor sculpture in the surrounding plaza. Another fine sculpture garden across Jefferson Drive displays more than 60 pieces of large-scale contemporary work *(see p40)*. *7th St, at Independence Ave, SW • Map Q5 • 202-633-4674 • Open 10am–5:30pm daily • Dis. access • Free*

The Federal Triangle

The area now known as the Federal Triangle was developed during Franklin D. Roosevelt's administration and improved by John F. Kennedy. Before then, the three-sided site, between 6th and 14th Streets and Pennsylvania and Constitution Avenues NW, was a run-down area. Its main buildings are the Federal Trade Commission, the National Archives, the Department of Justice, the Internal Revenue Service, and the R. Reagan Building and International Trade Center.

6 National Museum of Natural History

A favorite with children, yet filled with fascinating displays and artifacts that appeal to everyone, the vast halls of this Smithsonian museum have everything from the tiny bones of a snake to a giant ritual statue from Easter Island. Other exhibits include the vast Mammal Hall, Pacific Island canoes, fabulous gemstones (including the Hope Diamond), a giant squid, a scene from a Chinese opera, and an Egyptian mummy case *(see pp42 & 53)*.
Constitution Ave & 10th St, NW • Map P4 • Open 10am–5:30pm daily; Closed Dec 25 • Dis. access • Free

7 United States Holocaust Memorial Museum

Among the city's most challenging sites, this museum is both a working study center for issues relating to the Holocaust and a national memorial for the millions murdered by the World War II Nazi government. The museum is solemn and respectful while engrossing and highly informative. Free timed passes are required to view the three-story permanent exhibition. Passes can be obtained at the museum on the day of visit, or in advance online. There are some special exhibitions that can be seen without passes *(see p42)*.
100 Raoul Wallenberg Place, SW (14th St between Independence Ave & C St, SW) • Map P5 • 202-488-0400 • www.ushmm.org • Open 10am–5:30pm daily; Closed Yom Kippur, Dec 25 • Dis. access • Free

8 Washington Monument

The plain Egyptian design of this radiant spire was largely the result of congressional cost-cutting, but now it seems an inspired choice. At 555 ft (165 m), the monument, built to honor the first president of the United States, towers over everything in the neighborhood and is ringed by 50 flags representing the 50 states of America *(see p48)*. *15th St between Independence & Constitution Aves • Map P5 • Closed to the public due to damage sustained from the 2011 earthquake. Check www.nps.gov/wamo for more information • Dis. access • Free*

Washington Monument

9 Lincoln Memorial

This imposing marble memorial honors the US president who carried the country through its most difficult era. Designed by Henry Bacon (1866–1924) and featuring a monumental 19-ft (6-m) high statue of the seated Lincoln by Daniel Chester French (1850–1931), the memorial was dedicated in 1922.

Lincoln Memorial

The Greek architecture reflects the ideals of its time *(see p48)*. *23rd St, NW & Independence Ave • Map M5 • Open 24 hours*

10 Vietnam Veterans' Memorial

This stark remembrance features a black polished wall on which are carved the names of those who died during the Vietnam War. Controversial when it opened, because of its minimalism and because it failed to glorify the war, the memorial has become one of the world's most popular. Its creator, Maya Lin, was a 21-year-old Chinese-American student when she completed the design. More traditional statues were added in 1984 *(see p48)*. *Constitution Ave & 21st St, NW • Map M5 • Open 24 hours • Dis. access • Free*

Statues, Vietnam Veterans' Memorial

A Morning Walk by the Waterfront

Begin at the **Franklin D. Roosevelt Memorial** *(see p48)* on West Basin Drive. A Tourmobile stop *(see p117)* is directly in front of the memorial (parking is limited). The sweeping flow of this memorial carries visitors past waterscapes punctuated by engravings of the words of the president and evocative sculptures of his times.

On the left, leaving the memorial, is the little Japanese pagoda given to the city as a gesture of friendship by the mayor of Yokohama in 1958. Graceful Japanese cherry trees line the Tidal Basin bank beyond. Continue east across Inlet Bridge. About five minutes along the walkway stands the brilliant **Jefferson Memorial** *(see p48)*, noted for its delicate design in spite of its size. Looking out from the steps here to the city is a wonderful experience.

Continue around the waterfront, cross Outlet Bridge, and bear to the left to the little boathouse, where you can rent a paddleboat for a unique view of the Tidal Basin *(Open 10am–4pm daily; last boats out at 5pm • Adm)*. If you prefer to stay on dry ground, continue north toward the **Washington Monument** and cross Maine Avenue leading to Raoul Wallenberg Place. On the right is the **US Holocaust Memorial Museum**. Before taking in the exhibits, gird yourself with some kosher fare in the **Museum Café** *(see p85)*. Then spend the afternoon in remembrance of lives tragically lost under the Nazi regime.

Following pages: **The Washington Monument at sunset**

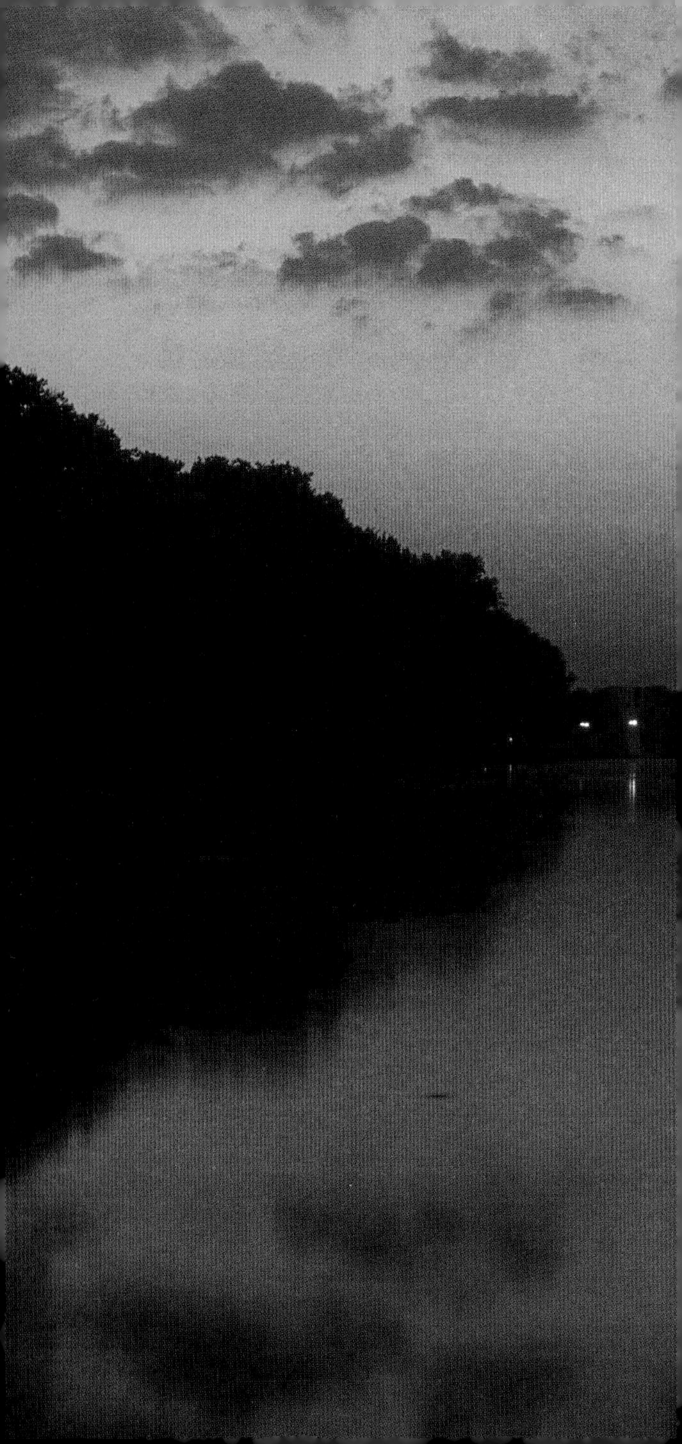

Left **World War II Memorial** Right **National Archives façade**

TOP 10 Best of the Rest

1 World War II Memorial

This memorial includes 12 bas-relief sculptures depicting America at war. Inscriptions at the base of the fountains mark key battles *(see p49)*.

2 Enid A. Haupt Garden

These formal gardens contrast scale, color, and scent *(see p50)*. *1050 Independence Ave, SW • Map P5 • Open daily • Dis. access • Free*

3 National Archives of the United States

Home to foundation documents of the nation, including the Declaration of Independence. *700 Pennsylvania Ave, NW • Map Q4 • 202-357-5000 • Open 10am–5:30pm daily (to 7pm in summer) • Dis. access • Free*

4 Franklin D. Roosevelt Memorial

The inclusion of FDR's dog in the statuary indicates the human scale of this tribute *(see p48)*. *900 Ohio Dr, SW • Map N6 • Open 24 hours • Dis. access • Free*

5 Jefferson Memorial

Words of the Declaration of Independence are engraved on the wall here *(see p48)*. *Tidal Basin • Map N6 • Open 24 hours daily • Dis. access • Free*

6 National Museum of the American Indian

This museum is a national center for Native American culture *(see p42)*. *4th St and Independence Ave, SW • Map Q5 • Open 10am–5:30pm daily*

7 Korean War Veterans Memorial

The 19 stainless steel sculptures in this memorial to the 1953 Korean "police action" wrenchingly evoke the realities of war. *21st St & Independence Ave, SW • Map M5 • Open 24 hours • Dis. access • Free*

8 Bureau of Engraving and Printing

See millions of dollars being printed as you walk along the gallery overlooking the production floor. *14th St at C St, SW • Map P5 • 202-874-2330 • www.moneyfactory.org for tour info • Open 8:30am–3:30pm Mon–Fri • Dis. access • Free*

9 National Museum of African Art

A program of changing exhibitions highlights a diverse collection of African pieces. *950 Independence Ave, SW • Map Q5 • Open 10am–5:30pm daily • Dis. access • Free*

10 Old Post Office Pavilion

The view from the tower here is among the finest in the city. A food court and shops draw hordes of visitors *(see p57)*. *Tower: open Apr–Aug: 10am–8pm Mon–Sat, noon–7pm Sun; Sep–Mar: 10am–7pm Mon–Sat • Dis. access • Free*

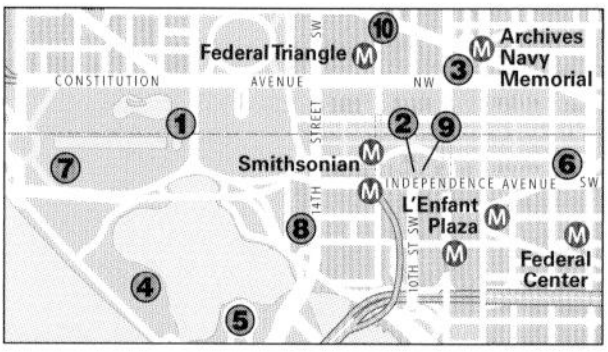

Left **Smithsonian Teddy Bears** Right **National Air and Space Museum store**

TOP 10 Items in Museum Stores

1 Smithsonian Teddy Bear
This is the Smithsonian's commemorative version of the Ideal Toy Company's 1902 bear, based on a famous *Washington Star* cartoon showing "Teddy" Roosevelt with a bear cub. In the National Museum of American History *(see pp18–19)*.

2 Jackie Kennedy Jewels
Who needs the real thing when reproductions of Jackie's most famous pieces can be purchased for next to nothing at the museum store at the National Museum of American History *(see pp18–19)*.

3 Ceramic Teapots
Ceramic teapots in various colors, styles, and sizes. The most popular are the decorative mini teapots. In the National Museum of Natural History *(see p78)*.

4 Spy Gadgets
Everything a budding spy might require can be found at the International Spy Museum store. Among the array of goodies are false noses and mustaches to "How To" guides *(see p54)*.

5 Leather Flight Jackets
Good-quality leather jackets recreate the genuine flying jackets, and the selection and prices are reasonable. In the National Air and Space Museum *(see pp16–17)*.

6 Inkshuk Sculptures
Sculptures, carvings, ceramic pots, and plates created in intricate Native American designs. In the Museum of the American Indian *(see p77)*.

7 NASA Space Suits
Miniature orange suits, created with care and precise attention to detail, are available for little astronauts. In the National Air and Space Museum *(see pp16–17)*.

8 Geodes and Fossils
The Gem and Mineral store has beautiful examples of geodes – sparkling crystals grown within hollows of other stones – and of fossils embedded in various matrixes. In the National Museum of Natural History *(see p78)*.

9 Chrysanthemum Satin Kimono
One of the many magnificent fabric creations available at these two Oriental museum stores. They also have unusual novelties such as *haiku* refrigerator magnets. In the Freer Gallery of Art and Arthur M. Sackler Gallery *(see p41)*.

10 Handmade Crafts
The Textile Museum's beautiful range of shawls and scarves, vibrant handbags, cute felt dolls, and inspiring textile-related books all make lovely gifts *(see p43)*.

Left **Dinosaur Hall** Center **Insect Zoo** Right **"How Things Fly"**

Top 10 Children's Attractions

1 Johnson IMAX Theater
The movie screen at the Museum of Natural History is 66 ft high and 90 ft wide (20 m x 28 m), and some of the films shown are 3-D using polarized glasses. Subjects include dinosaurs and the ocean *(see p78)*.

2 Smithsonian Carousel
This lovely carousel with its fancifully carved steeds is a treat for young and old alike. The sounds of the band organ are very cheering. *1000 Jefferson Dr, SW • Map P5 • Open 10am–5:30pm daily weather permitting • Adm*

3 O. Orkin Insect Zoo
Live arthropods scamper and creep in this section of the Museum of Natural History – some can also be held *(see p78)*.

4 "How Things Fly"
Highly interactive exhibits and scheduled demonstrations at the National Air and Space Museum explain the principles that make flight possible. Kids can understand natural animal flight and human flight in contraptions from balloons to the space shuttle *(see pp16–17)*.

5 Children's Film Program at the National Gallery of Art
Animations, environmental and nature films, and child's-eye views of life are compiled into lively shows the right length for children's attention spans *(see pp20–23)*.

6 Invention at Play
This engaging exhibition in the Museum of American History explores the impact play has on invention. The award-winning exposition has a family-friendly design and is a great way to fritter away a few hours *(see p18)*.

7 Ice Skating
The fountain in the National Gallery of Art Sculpture Garden *(see p23)* is frozen for ice skating in the winter, and visitors can rent skates on site.

8 Dinosaur Hall
Many kids make their first contact with the study of the natural world through their fascination with dinosaurs. The displays at the National Museum of Natural History should wow them – as will the stunning mammal exhibit *(see p78)*.

9 Newseum
While a news museum might not seem an obvious choice for kids, activities like recording a news segment in the NBC interactive gallery usually prove a big hit *(see p87)*.

10 Einstein Planetarium
Astronomy is kid-friendly at the Air and Space Museum in "One World One Sky: Big Bird's Adventure". The free, 20-minute show takes place on Fridays and the first consecutive Saturday and Sunday of the month. Book tickets in advance *(see p16)*.

Price Categories

For a three-course meal for one with half a bottle of wine (or equivalent meal), taxes, and extra charges.	
$	under $30
$$	$30–$50
$$$	$50–$75
$$$$	$75–$100
$$$$$	over $100

Above **Atrium Café**

TOP 10 Lunch Spots

1 Cascade Café & Gelato Bar

Behind a glass wall in the National Gallery of Art concourse is a man-made waterfall. Facing this view is an attractive café with a wide range of hot and cold food. *3–7th St & Constitution Ave, NW • Map Q4 • 202-712-7458 • Dis. access • $*

2 Paul Bakery and Café

An outlet of the famous French bakery, this café offers a wide variety of sandwiches, snacks, desserts, and organic breads. *801 Pennsylvania Ave, NW • Map Q4 • 202-524-4500 • $*

3 Mitsitam Café

Meaning "Let's eat"in Piscataway. The menu is inspired by Native Americans. *National Museum of American Indian, 4th St & Independence Ave, SW • Map Q5 • 202-633-1000 • Dis. access • $*

4 Garden Café

This little restaurant in the National Gallery of Art has the choice of a good buffet or a traditional à la carte menu. Surroundings of greenery combine with lofty ceilings. *3–7th St and Constitution Ave, NW • Map Q4 • 202-712-7458 • Dis. access • $*

5 The Source

An Asian-influenced menu. The three-course, fixed-price lunch menu is recommended. Enjoy a casual dining atmosphere at this Newseum location. *575 Pennsylvania Ave, NW • Map Q4 • 202-637-6100 • $$$*

6 Pavilion Café

Sandwiches, salads, pizzas, and a variety of desserts are served in the Sculpture Garden at the National Gallery of Art. *7th St and Constitution Ave, NW • Map Q4 • 202-289-3360 • Dis. access • $*

7 United States Holocaust Memorial Museum

The Museum Café serves traditional, kosher, and contemporary American favorites *(see p78)*.

8 Reagan International Trade Center Food Court

This large food court has Texas grill, sushi, and dim sum as specialities. Photo ID is required for adults to enter the building. *1300 Pennsylvania Ave, NW • Map Q4 • 202-312-1300 • Dis. access • $*

9 Michel Richard Central

Celebrity chef Michel Richard serves up French flavors and American concoctions like lobster burgers and faux *foie gras*. *1001 Pennsylvania Ave, NW • Map P4 • 202-626-0015 • $$$*

10 Atrium Café

The Museum of Natural History's atrium café serves natural, sustainable foods *(see p78)*.

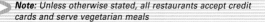

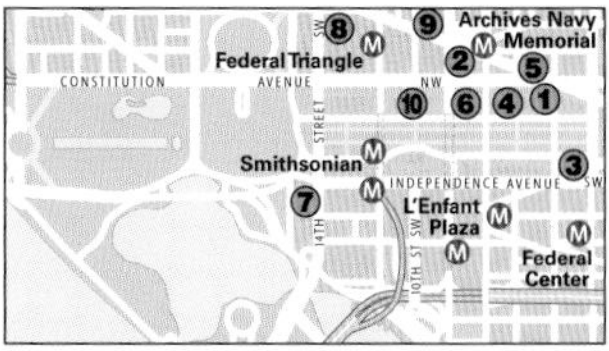

Note: *Unless otherwise stated, all restaurants accept credit cards and serve vegetarian meals*

Left **Willard Hotel** Right **US Navy Memorial**

Penn Quarter

LIKE OTHER URBAN DOWNTOWN AREAS, *Washington's city center is filled with shops, hotels, restaurants, and theaters for every taste. Yet downtown Washington borders Pennsylvania Avenue – often called "America's main street." This is the direct route between the White House and the Capitol, and is therefore rich in historic associations. Presidential inauguration parades sweep down the avenue every four years; citizens protest here; President Lincoln was shot and died nearby. Washington's importance to world culture is reflected in the ease with which local restaurants and stores cater to an international clientele. The area draws visitors to the attractions of Chinatown, the Verizon Center, and the feeling of being at the center of the political world.*

TOP 10 Sights

1. Ford's Theater
2. Verizon Center
3. Newseum
4. National Building Museum
5. National Museum of Women in the Arts
6. National Aquarium
7. Chinatown
8. Willard Hotel
9. National Portrait Gallery
10. US Navy Memorial

Newseum building

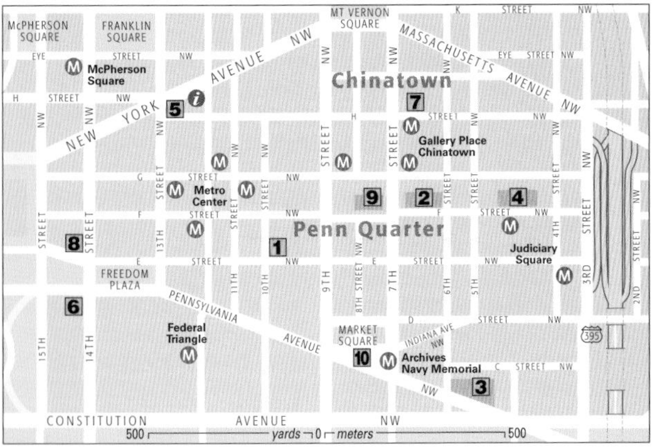

Ford's Theater

1 Ford's Theater

John Wilkes Booth shot Abraham Lincoln in a balcony box here on April 14, 1865 – a tragic event that has made Ford's Theater one of America's best-known historical sites. A museum contains Booth's .44 caliber Derringer pistol and other objects and information giving insights into Lincoln and the assassination plot. The restored building also houses theater productions. Directly across 10th Street is Petersen House, where Lincoln died after being carried from the theater *(see p44)*. *511 10th St, NW • Map Q4 • Open 9am–5pm daily • 202-347-4833 • Dis. access • Free*

2 Verizon Center

While the Verizon Center is principally a sports arena, it has also become an unofficial community center. It draws crowds night after night with college and professional sports events, big-name concerts, circuses, figure skating performances, and other events *(see p52)*. *601 F St, NW • Map Q4 • Dis. access*

3 Newseum

An awe-inspiring dissection of 500 years of the press. Visitors are able to compare media freedoms in 190 countries and view enlarged front pages from around the world that are updated daily. The 9/11 gallery and that of Pulitzer Prize photography are particularly moving. An unmissable museum experience *(see p43)*. *555 Pennsylvania Ave, NW • Map P4 • Open 9am–5pm daily • 202-292-6100 • www.newseum.org • Dis. access • Adm*

4 National Building Museum

This grand structure would be a fabulous place to visit even if it were empty. Its eight massive interior columns are among the largest in the world, and its immense interior space has beautiful natural light. The museum itself is dedicated to documenting and displaying important themes in the art and craft of building structures. It has permanent exhibitions on the city of Washington and on art created from tools, and mounts a stream of temporary exhibitions on topics such as the growth of urban transit and the development of architectural and construction methods. Other exhibits highlight the work of individual prominent architects. Families will particularly enjoy the Building Zone, where kids will be kept amused building towers and driving toy bulldozers. *401 F St, NW • Map Q4 • Open 10am–4pm Mon–Sat, 11am–4pm Sun • www.nbm.org • Dis. access • Free, $5 donation recommended*

Great Hall, National Building Museum

National Museum of Women in the Arts

5 National Museum of Women in the Arts

The collection of works by female artists here is among the world's best, ranging from Lavinia Fontana's *Portrait of a Noblewoman* (c.1580) to Frida Kahlo's 1937 *Self-Portrait Dedicated to Leon Trotsky (see p41).* *1250 New York Ave, NW • Map P3 • 202-783-5000 • Open 10am–5pm Mon–Sat, noon–5pm Sun • Dis. access • Adm*

6 National Aquarium

One of the oldest aquariums in the world (1873). Sharks, alligators, piranha, and more than 300 other species are housed here *(see p53).* *14th St between Pennsylvania & Constitution Aves, NW • Map P4 • 202-482-2825 • Open 9am–5pm daily; Closed Thanksgiving, Dec 25 • Dis. access • Adm (no credit cards)*

7 Chinatown

Chinese culture abounds here, with an array of restaurants and shops. A Chinese arch was funded by Beijing and constructed in 1986, with seven pagoda-style roofs ornamented with 300 dragons. *7th & H Sts, NW • Map Q3*

8 Willard Hotel

A glorious center of historic and political Washington. Every US president, beginning with Franklin Pierce in 1853, has stayed as a guest or attended functions here. When Lincoln was inaugurated in March 1861, there were already assassination threats. Detective Alan Pinkerton smuggled him into the Willard, and presidential business was conducted before the fireplace in the lobby. *1401 Pennsylvania Ave, NW • Map P4 • Dis. access*

Pennsylvania Avenue

When the federal government moved to the city in 1800, Pennsylvania Avenue was selected as the "main street" because the area to the south was too muddy after rains, and the avenue offered a direct route from the President's House to the Capitol – the only substantial buildings in town.

9 National Portrait Gallery

The ornate 1836 building is a masterpiece in itself. The gallery celebrates remarkable Americans through visual and performing arts. Permanent exhibitions focus on individuals who have helped to shape the country's culture, from presidents and poets to villains and activists. *8th & F Sts, NW • Map Q4 • Open 11:30am–7pm daily • Dis. access • Free*

10 US Navy Memorial

The centerpiece of this delightful public space is a granite floor – a huge map of the world surrounded by fountains. A statue, dubbed "The Lone Sailor," overlooks the expanse *(see p49).* A free film shows daily at noon. *701 Pennsylvania Ave, NW • Map Q4 • Open 9:30–5pm daily • Dis. access • Free*

Archway, Chinatown

Price Categories

For a three-course meal for one with half a bottle of wine (or equivalent meal), taxes and extra charges.

$	under $30
$$	$30–$50
$$$	$50–$75
$$$$	$75–$100
$$$$$	over $100

Left **Jaleo** Right **Old Ebbitt Grill**

TOP 10 Places to Eat

1 Proof
Wine-lovers are drawn to this downtown hotspot known for its creative cuisine and wine menu. *775 G St, NW • Map Q3 • 202-737-7663 • $$$*

2 Jaleo
A fine *tapas* restaurant, Jaleo draws raves for its egg-plant flan and sautéed shrimp. The atmosphere is lively, with great music and plenty of sangria. *480 7th St, NW • Map Q4 • 202-628-7949 • Dis. access • $$*

3 Old Ebbitt Grill
A pub-style restaurant with great hamburgers and seasonal entrées. Oyster bar in season. *675 15th St, NW • Map P4 • 202-347-4800 • Dis. access • $$*

4 Café Atlantico
Creative Caribbean, Spanish, and Central American dishes sparkle here and the atmosphere is good fun. The wine list is exceptional, and service is of very high quality. *405 8th St, NW • Map Q4 • 202-393-0812 • Dis. access • $$$*

5 Elephant and Castle
Traditional British comfort food is served here in a homely pub-style atmosphere: roast beef-filled yorkshire puddings, sausage and mash, and shepherd's pie are among the favorites. *1201 Pennsylvania Ave, NW • Map P4 • 202-347-7707 • Dis. access • $$*

6 Brasserie Beck
A paradise for beer lovers, Beck offers several varieties and a large French-Belgian menu. *1101 K St NW • Map Q3 • 202-408-1717 • $$$*

7 Full Kee
This Chinatown restaurant serves outstanding soups at an open station. *509 H St, NW • Map Q3 • 202-371-2233 • $$*

8 Ceiba
Haceinda chic interior and Nuevo-Latino themed food. *701 14th St, NW • Map P4 • 202-393-3983 • Dis. access • $$$*

9 Tony Cheng's Mongolian Restaurant
The ground floor of this restaurant focuses on Mongolian-style barbecue while Cantonese cuisine and dim sum are served on the second floor. *619 H St, NW • Map Q4 • 202-371-8669 • $$*

10 District Chophouse and Brewery
This bar and restaurant caters to sports fans from the Verizon Center. *509 7th St, NW • Map Q4 • 202-347-3434 • Dis. access • $$$*

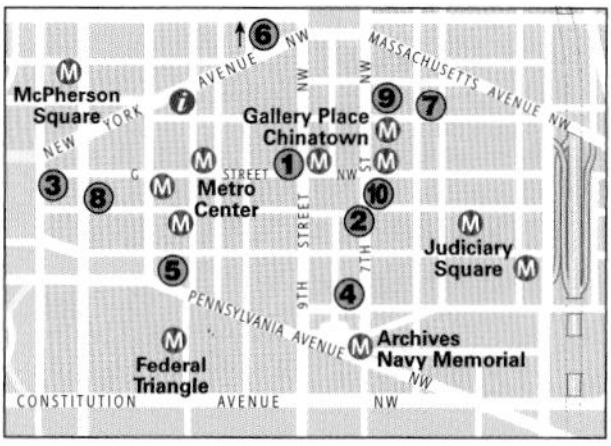

Note: *Unless otherwise stated, all restaurants accept credit cards and serve vegetarian meals*

Left **Organization of American States** Center **The White House** Right **Kennedy Center**

The White House and Foggy Bottom

THE MAJESTIC WHITE HOUSE CLEARLY DEFINES *this area of the city – everyday business in Washington frequently takes place around the house because the major east-west routes, Pennsylvania and Constitution Avenues, are close by. Many government buildings stand in the vicinity, including the old and new Executive Office Buildings, the Federal Reserve Building, and the State and Treasury Departments. To the west lies Foggy Bottom, a former swamp area now home to George Washington University. Farther west, the Kennedy Center stands on the waterfront. Throughout the area, as one would expect, restaurants, hotels, and shops provide the quality of service required by high-profile diplomats and politicians.*

TOP 10 Sights

1. The White House
2. Kennedy Center
3. Corcoran Gallery of Art
4. Renwick Gallery
5. Eisenhower Executive Office Building
6. Treasury Building
7. Octagon
8. Organization of American States
9. Daughters of the American Revolution
10. Federal Reserve Building

Corcoran Gallery statue

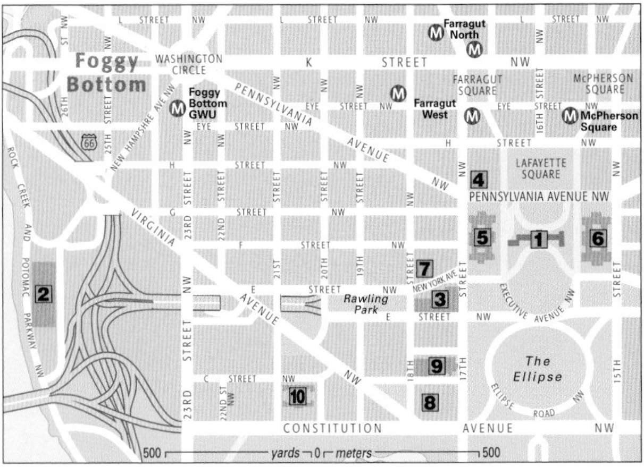

1 The White House

Beautiful from any angle, the White House is a symbol of US political power and of democracy throughout the world *(see pp12–15)*.

2 Kennedy Center

A memorial to President John F. Kennedy, this huge performance complex – the largest in the country – presents the best expressions of the artistic culture he loved so well. National and international stars perform opera, concerts, musical comedy, drama, jazz, dance, and ballet. Located overlooking the Potomac, its terraces and rooftop restaurant have dazzling views *(see p58)*. ✆ *New Hampshire Ave at Rock Creek Parkway, NW • Map M4 • 202-467-4600 • Dis. access*

3 Corcoran Gallery of Art

This 1897 building is among the finest Beaux Arts designs in the United States. Note the atrium with its symmetrical stairway. The art collection inside includes some of the very best of American and European masterworks. In the American art collection, works by the Hudson River School and the Luminists are especially strong *(see p40)*. ✆ *500 17th St, NW • Map N4 • 202-639-1700 • Open 10am–5pm Wed–Mon (until 9pm Thu), closed federal holidays; guided tours noon • Dis. access • Adm*

4 Renwick Gallery

This Smithsonian museum is a gem, with its displays of fine American craft works and American art. The second-floor Grand Salon served as a ballroom and site for special events when the Corcoran Gallery was located here before 1897. The 1859 structure, named after its

Renwick Gallery entrance detail

architect, James Renwick, Jr, is a marvelous Second Empire-style building *(see p40)*. ✆ *1661 Pennsylvania Ave, NW • Map N3 • 202-633-7970 • Open 10am–5:30pm daily; Closed Dec 25 • Free • Dis. access*

5 Dwight D. Eisenhower Executive Office Building

This is another Second Empire building, but on a mammoth scale. Many people consider its highly embellished style and daunting proportions – 300,000 sq ft (27,871 sq m) of office space on five stories – to be magnificent, but others agree with esteemed U.S. author Mark Twain (1835–1910) and consider it to be "the ugliest building in America." The Departments of State, Navy, and War were housed here on its completion in 1888. Today it houses the majority of offices for White House staff. Tours are suspended indefinitely. ✆ *17th St and Pennsylvania Ave, NW • Map N4 • 202-395-5895*

Eisenhower Executive Office Building

George Washington University

For the last 50 years, GWU has been a major presence in Foggy Bottom, contributing to its diversity and filling its streets with the energy of young students. Founded as Columbian College in 1821, the school adopted its current name in 1904 to honor the wishes expressed by George Washington for the establishment of a major university in the city.

6 Treasury Building

The Greek-Revival style of this old building, designed in 1833, suggests a Temple of Money, and the imposing interior design confirms the seriousness with which the republic has always treated its currency. The restored Salmon P. Chase Suite and the Andrew Johnson Office reflect the gravity of official actions during and after the Civil War. The burglar-proof vault is always a hit with visitors because of the beauty of its cast-iron walls and its demonstration of the low security needs of a simpler day *(see p45)*. *1500 Pennsylvania Ave, NW • Map P4 • Tours currently only available for citizens and legal residents of the US, by appt only: 202-622-2000*

7 The Octagon Museum

This unique and graceful building houses the oldest architecture museum in the country. The house was completed in 1801 – one of the first private residences to be built to Pierre L'Enfant's plan – and provided shelter to President James Madison and his family while workers were rebuilding the White House after its destruction during the War of 1812. The exhibitions of the museum focus especially on the early Federal period of architecture, principally from 1800 to 1830. It was designed by William Thornton, the original architect of the US Capitol, as a second home for John Tayloe III, a wealthy friend of George Washington *(see p45)*. *1799 New York Ave • Map N4 • 202-626-7439 • Self-guided tours are available Thu & Fri from 1–4pm. • Dis. access*

The Octagon Museum

8 Organization of American States

The OAS's beautiful building, with its three round-topped arches, is one of the area's architectural delights. The OAS Art Museum of the Americas has a permanent collection of Western Hemisphere art that is one of the most important in the US. The Organization of American States is a cooperative association of all 35 countries of the hemisphere to promote economic development, protect human rights, and strengthen democracy. *17th St at Constitution Ave, NW • Map N4 • 202-458-6016 • Museum: 201 18th St, NW; Open 10am–5pm Tue–Sun; closed Federal holidays • Free*

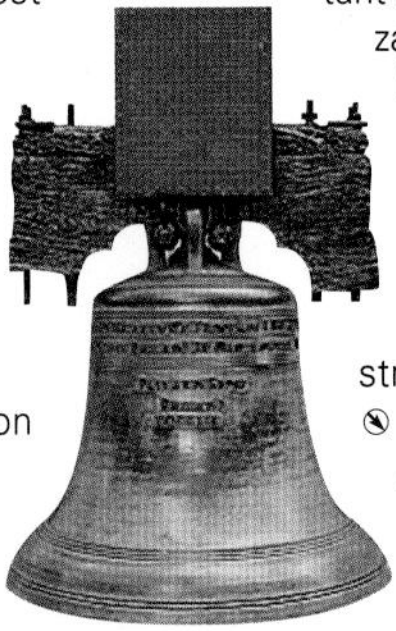

Liberty Bell, Treasury Building

9 Daughters of the American Revolution

The largest concert hall in the city is in Constitution Hall, the grand performance space operated by the Daughters of the American Revolution (DAR). The cornerstone of this John Russell Pope design was laid in 1928, using the same trowel George Washington used for the US Capitol building cornerstone in 1793. The DAR also has a fascinating museum of early American artifacts, ranging from a simple 17th-century dwelling to an elaborate Victorian parlor. The DAR is a volunteer women's service promoting patriotism, history, and education. Any woman who can prove lineal descent from a patriot of the American Revolution is eligible to join. *1776 D St, NW • Map N4 • 202-628-1776 • Museum: Open 9:30am– 4pm Mon–Fri, 9am–5pm Sat; Closed 2 weeks in July • Free*

10 Federal Reserve Building (Eccles Building)

Another gleaming white design by Paul P. Cret, architect of the Folger Shakespeare Library *(see p71)*. The Federal Reserve System is the central banking authority in the United States, regulating and facilitating banking and the flow of currency and financial transactions. *2001 C St, NW • Map N4*

Federal Reserve Building

A Day Exploring 17th Street NW

Morning

Begin your day with a tour of **Decatur House** *(see p44)*, a gorgeous Neo-Classical mansion. After the tour, turn left and walk to the end of the block; turn left onto 17th St, NW, and continue one block to Pennsylvania Ave. The **Renwick Gallery** *(see p91)* is on the corner. Don't miss the luxurious ballroom on the second floor.

Continuing east on Pennsylvania, you can view the renowned north portico of **The White House** *(see pp12–15)* on your right. Reverse direction, return to 17th St, and turn left to take in the ornate **Eisenhower Executive Office Building** *(see p91)*.

A block south is **Corcoran Gallery of Art** *(see p91)*, with its superb American and European art. Lunch at **Todd Gray's Muse** (closed Mon & Tue) *(see p97)*, in its Beaux Arts atrium.

Afternoon

After leaving the Corcoran, turn right and continue down 17th Street one block, to D Street. Turn right, and almost at the end of the block is the entrance of the **Daughters of the American Revolution**. In addition to the fascinating period rooms, the gift shop is a treat for anyone with an interest in quilting, samplers, or porcelain.

End your day by hailing a taxi on 17th Street to the **Kennedy Center** *(see p91)* and enjoy dinner at the **Roof Terrace Restaurant** *(see p97)*, with its stunning river views.

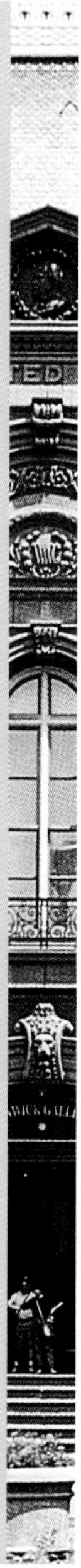

Left **Benedict Arnold** Right **Watergate Senate Commitee**

TOP 10 Political Scandals

1 Benedict Arnold
Arnold, in the early years of the Revolution, was an effective military leader on the colonists' side. Yet, driven by money, he conspired to turn over to the British the army installation at West Point. His name became synonymous with "traitor."

2 Thomas Jefferson and Sally Hemings
The press commented in the early 1800s that Jefferson had had an affair and borne children with his slave, Sally Hemings. Jefferson denied the accusations, but now DNA evidence makes the connection probable.

3 Andrew Jackson and the Petticoat Affair
Margaret Eaton, wife of President Jackson's secretary of war, was rumored to have had a scandalous past. Jackson defended her honor and his enemies attacked, threatening his presidency.

4 "Boss" Shepherd
Alexander Shepherd pushed the Board of Public Works to great accomplishments in the 1870s, but he was later run out of town for bankrupting city government.

5 Whiskey Ring
In 1875 it was revealed that liquor taxes were being evaded by distillers and the officials they bribed. There were 110 convictions. President Grant secured the acquittal of his private secretary.

6 Teapot Dome
The oil fields at Teapot Dome, Wyoming, had been set aside as a reserve for the US Navy. In the 1920s, oil interests bribed government officials to lease the land to them, without competitive bidding.

7 Watergate
In 1972, President Nixon's re-election workers broke into the Democrats' Watergate offices planning to gather campaign information. Their arrest, and the effort to contain the scandal, forced Nixon to resign in 1974.

8 Wilbur Mills and Fanne Fox
Mills, chairman of the powerful House Ways and Means Committee, was caught frolicking with his friend, stripper Fanne Fox. He was forced to resign in 1974.

9 Iran-Contra Affair
In the 1980s, Ronald Reagan's administration carried out plans to secretly sell US weapons to Iran and use the proceeds to support Nicaraguan rebels. The investigation revealed deception and corruption.

10 Bill Clinton and Monica Lewinsky
Clinton's denial of sexual relations with the White House intern led to charges of perjury, obstruction of justice, and an investigation by the House of Representatives.

For places of politics and and intrigue **See pp54–5**

Left **Kinkeads** Right **Blue Duck Tavern**

Price Categories

For a three-course meal for one with half a bottle of wine (or equivalent meal), taxes and extra charges.

$	under $30
$$	$30–$50
$$$	$50–$75
$$$$	$75–$100
$$$$$	over $100

TOP 10 Places to Eat

1 Blue Duck Tavern

Chef Brian McBride's specialties are prepared before your eyes in an open kitchen. Must-try dishes include thick fries cooked in duck fat and mini apple pies. *1201 24th St, NW • Map M3 • 202-419-6755 • $$$*

2 Kinkeads

Good American cooking with an emphasis on fresh seafood. Live piano music on Friday and Saturday nights. *2000 Pennsylvania Ave, NW • Map N3 • 202-296-7700 • Dis. access • $$$*

3 Equinox

A showplace for fresh local ingredients, Equinox is a pioneer in sustainable cooking. The menu is seasonal and features many organic ingredients. *818 Connecticut Ave NW • Map N3 • 202-331-8118 • $$$$*

4 Georgia Brown's

Southern cooking with very generous portions of both food and attention. Chicken, fish, stews, corn bread, shrimp, and grits highlight the menu. *950 15th St, NW • Map P3 • 202-393-4499 • Dis. access • $$*

5 Marcel's

Award-winning French and Flemish cuisine, including crispy skate wing and Carolina pheasant, wins rave reviews. Pre-theater menu available for $55. *2401 Pennsylvania Ave, NW • Map M3 • 202-296-1166 • $$$$*

6 Circle Bistro

Close to Kennedy Center and a great spot for pre-theater dinner and drinks. *1 Washington Cir • Map M3 • 202-872-1680 • Dis. access • $$*

7 Primi Piatti

A northern Italian restaurant with fine lamb dishes and other staples. *2013 I St, NW • Map N3 • 202-223-3600 • $$*

8 Roof Terrace Restaurant

At the Kennedy Center *(see p91)*, this elegant restaurant has unrivaled views. Specialties change every season. *New Hampshire Ave at Rock Creek Parkway, NW • Map M4 • 202-416-8555 • Dis. access • $$*

9 Prime Rib

Steaks and chops dominate, also seafood and a vegetable platter. Jacket required for men. *2020 K St, NW • Map N3 • 202-466-8811 • Closed Sun • Dis. access • $$$$*

10 Todd Gray's Muse

In the atrium of the Corcoran Gallery *(see p91)*. Sunday brunch with live music. *500 17th St, NW • Map N4 • 202-639-1786 • Closed Mon & Tue • Dis. access • $*

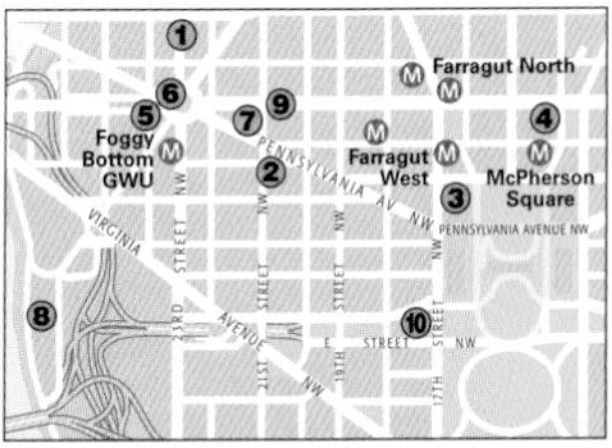

***Note:** Unless otherwise stated, all restaurants accept credit cards and serve vegetarian meals*

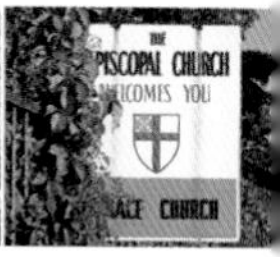

Left **Tudor Place** Center **M Street** Right **Grace Church**

Georgetown

WHEN ABIGAIL ADAMS ARRIVED IN WASHINGTON *in 1800, she described Georgetown as "the very dirtiest hole I ever saw." Then a major port with a huge slave and tobacco trade, cheap housing, and commercial wharves, the town may have been unattractive. But the Chesapeake and Ohio Canal and its competitor, the Baltimore and Ohio Railroad, brought prosperity to Georgetown, and therefore style. When the canal began to fail after flood damage, slum conditions returned, until Franklin D. Roosevelt partly rehabilitated the area. Its current modish position stems from the Kennedy era, when Georgetown became fashionable.*

Georgetown University

Top 10 Sights

1. **Dumbarton Oaks Museum and Gardens**
2. **Washington Harbour**
3. **Chesapeake and Ohio Canal**
4. **M Street and Wisconsin Avenue**
5. **N Street**
6. **Georgetown University**
7. **Grace Church**
8. **Old Stone House**
9. **Tudor Place**
10. **Oak Hill Cemetery**

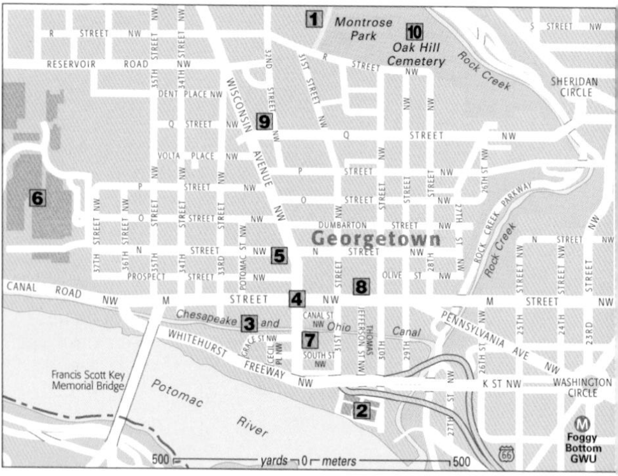

Rowhouses, C&O Canal

1 Dumbarton Oaks Museum and Gardens

This elegant Federal-style house, with its Philip Johnson-designed wing, houses a world-renowned collection of Byzantine and pre-Columbian artifacts. El Greco's *Visitation* is here also, possibly the Spanish master's last painting. The house and museum are surrounded by acres of gorgeous landscaping *(see p50)*. *1703 32nd St, NW • Map L1 • 202-339-6401 • Museum open 2–5pm Tue–Sun; Gardens open Mar–Oct: 2–6pm Tue–Sun • Free*

2 Washington Harbour

Dockside cafés, good restaurants, lovely views of the Potomac and the Kennedy Center, the Watergate complex, the Thompson boathouse, walkways for strolling, and benches for resting make the harbor a magnet for George-towners. The Washington Harbour residential and commercial building is an architectural exuberance designed by Arthur Cotton Moore and Associates. *3000–20 K St, NW, at the bottom of Thomas Jefferson St, NW (between 30th & 31st Sts) • Map L3*

Elegant Georgetown House

3 Chesapeake and Ohio Canal

Like so many features of the area, the C&O Canal grew from a dream of George Washington's as a gateway to commerce with the west ("west" meaning Ohio at the time). Coal, flour, fur, timber, whiskey, iron ore, and other goods traveled on barges, towed by mules walking along canalside paths. The canal's commercial days are over, but its entire length from Georgetown to Maryland has been turned into one of the most beloved national parks. Visitors can experience the beauty and serenity of the canal by walking about a block south from M Street, NW and turning west onto the towpath. The National Park Service Visitor Center for the C&O has terrific guidance for enjoying the canal. Guided tours and seasonal mule-powered barge rides are offered *(see p51)*. *Visitor Center: 1057 Thomas Jefferson St, NW • Map L3 • 202-653-5190 • Open 9am–4:30pm Wed–Sun; Closed winter*

4 M Street and Wisconsin Avenue

This intersection is surrounded by the main shopping, entertainment, dining, and bar-crawling areas of Georgetown. The attractive shops of Georgetown Park *(see p56)* include hundreds of retailers selling cool urban clothes, jewelry, fine wine, art and antiques, and countless other specialties. Restaurant food of every description is available, from modern gourmet to street window kebabs. *Map L2*

Metro Connection and Bus

Georgetown has no Metrorail station, and it used to be difficult for visitors to get to attractions here without a long walk from the nearest stations or a taxi ride. The Georgetown Metro Connection has been created to alleviate the problem. Running every 10 minutes daily, the shuttle bus provides inexpensive and convenient transportation to 13 locations from the Rosslyn and Dupont Circle metro stations. The Circulator Bus also runs every 5–10 minutes from 7am–9pm daily *(see p117).*

5 N Street

Little attractions and oddities abound on this street, which is noted for its exemplary architecture. Best seen from the sidewalk on 28th Street, NW, the house at No. 2726 has an outstanding mosaic by Marc Chagall, a friend of the former owner. The elegant Federal house at No. 3038 was home to Ambassador Averill Harriman, who lent the house to Jacqueline Kennedy after her husband's assassination. She later bought the elaborate 1794 Thomas Beall house across the street. Lessons in 19th-century architecture can be learned from the Federal houses at Nos. 3327 and 3339, the Second-Empire home at No. 3025–7, and the Victorian homes of Wheatley Row at Nos. 3041–45. ⊗ *Map L2*

N Street house

6 Georgetown University

This venerable institution sits on its hill overlooking Georgetown and the Potomac like a medieval citadel, its stone towers seemingly brooding with age. Yet the university is one of the most progressive in the country. Among the many interesting buildings here is the 1875 Healy Hall, built in an elaborate Flemish Renaissance style with surprising spiral adornment. Visitors can obtain campus maps and suggestions for strolls from the booth at the main gates. ⊗ *Gatehouse visitors booth: O & 37th Sts, NW • Map K2 • Opening hours vary depending on the university schedule. Call for details: 202-687-8299*

7 Grace Church

The 1866 church construction was built to house a congregation founded to serve the boatmen and support staff of the C&O Canal. The simple but extremely elegant design brings back the mid-19th century, although admittedly without the raucous bustle that must have accompanied the canal at its peak. The grounds are beautifully peaceful. The church offers poetry readings, theater performances, and concerts. Today's congregation has a serious devotion to community service and outreach. ⊗ *1041 Wisconsin Ave, NW (one block south of M St) • Map L3 • Open by appt (tel: 202-333-7100) • Office: Open 10am–6pm Mon, Tue, & Fri • Free*

For information on the Metro Connection, visit www.georgetowndc.com/shuttle.php or telephone 202-625-RIDE

Old Stone House

8 Old Stone House

This remarkable residence dating from 1766 looks a little incongruous standing directly in the heart of the shopping area, but it provides a captivating window into 18th-century life. The National Park Service provides tours and fascinating demonstrations of the crafts and tasks of colonial families. *3051 M St • Map L2 • 202-895-6070 • Open noon–5pm daily • Dis. access • Free*

9 Tudor Place

This house museum would be remarkable for its beauty even without its historic interest. Completed in 1816, the house was built by Thomas Peter, son of a Georgetown tobacco merchant, and Martha Custis Peter, granddaughter of Martha Washington. The Peter family occupied the house for six generations and hosted many prominent guests. *1644 31st St, NW • Map L2 • 202-965-0400 • Tours of the House: 10am–4pm Tue–Sat, noon–4pm Sun; Gardens: open 10am–4pm Tue–Sat, noon–4pm Sun; closed Jan, federal holidays • Dis. access • Adm*

10 Oak Hill Cemetery

The cemetery has a great diversity of graves and mausoleums in a Victorian garden setting. Its Gothic Revival chapel and the Van Ness Mausoleum are on the National Register of Historic Places. *3001 R St, NW • Map L1 • 202-337-2835 • Open 9am–4:30pm Mon–Fri, 1–4pm Sun, weather permitting*

A Morning in Georgetown

Begin at **Washington Harbour** *(see p99)* for its views of the Potomac right on the waterfront. Take a pleasant stroll along the river before heading up Thomas Jefferson Street, NW to the National Park Service Visitor Center for the **Chesapeake and Ohio Canal** *(see p99)*. In summer, mule-drawn barge rides are offered, with expert guides painting the historic background of the scenes before you.

Turn right and continue up Thomas Jefferson Street a short block and cross M Street, NW. In front of you is the **Old Stone House**, which has been lovingly preserved. National Park Service interpreters recreate some of the daily activities that might have taken place in the house in the 18th century.

Reverse direction and return down Thomas Jefferson Street to the canal. Turn right onto the towpath and stroll for two blocks until you reach an opening in the embankment. Follow the steps to the right to Wisconsin Avenue, NW. Cross the street to **Grace Church**. Enjoy the view of the lovely little church built for the spiritual needs of workers on the canal. The grounds, with their mature trees, make a relaxing rest spot. Recross Wisconsin Avenue and the canal to the shops at **Georgetown Park** *(see p104)*.

Before an afternoon of retail therapy, enjoy lunch at **Clyde's of Georgetown** *(see p105)* on level 3 or snack from the food court on level 1.

Following pages: **Georgetown rowhouses**

3005

Left & Center **Dean & DeLuca** Right **Window shopping, Georgetown**

TOP 10 Places to Shop

1 The Shops at Georgetown Park

In this large indoor mall right on the canal, shoppers can find the expected fashions, but also electrical goods, luggage, and many other specialties. There is a food court and popular restaurants *(see p56)*. *3222 M St, NW • Map L2 • Dis. access*

2 Dean & DeLuca

The New York-originated gourmet food store is about as luxurious as a grocery store can get. The salad bar is superb, and the ready-made meals have brought success to countless Georgetown dinner parties. *3276 M St, NW • Map L2 • Dis. access*

3 Appalachian Spring

This shop might as well be an informal museum, considering the quality of many of the hand-made crafts for sale. The quilts, carved wood, pottery, and fabrics would grace any setting. *1415 Wisconsin Ave, NW • Map L2*

4 The Phoenix

A charming store with contemporary clothing in natural fibers, classic jewelery, folk and fine art, and Mexican antiques. *1514 Wisconsin Ave, NW • Map L2*

5 Annie Creamcheese

Vintage clothes at reasonable prices are to be found here. A treasure trove of yesterday's trends. *3279 M St, NW • Map L2*

6 Proper Topper

Known for its selection of hats and accessories, this local favorite also stocks children's clothing and gift items. The store opens onto a garden courtyard that holds seasonal shopping events. There's a second location near Dupont Circle *3213 P St, NW • Map L2*

7 Jeweler's Werk Galerie

A showplace of handcrafted jewelry and wearable art, tucked away in Georgetown's Cadys Alley design enclave. The store is stocked with intricate necklaces, earrings and brooches by artists and designers. *3319 Cadys Alley • Map K3*

8 Bridge Street Books

Georgetown has few dedicated bookstores – this one is fertile ground for anyone with a serious interest in literature, history, film, politics, or poetry. *2814 Pennsylvania Ave, NW • Map L3*

9 Hu's Shoes

Visit this chic boutique for high-end women's shoes from emerging designers that you won't find in department stores. *3005 M St, NW • Map L3*

10 Georgetown Tobacco

A neighborhood fixture for more than 40 years, this quaint tobacco shop sells more than 100 brands of cigars, hand-sculpted pipes, and humidors. *3144 M St, NW • Map L3*

Price Categories

For a three-course meal for one with half a bottle of wine (or equivalent meal), taxes and extra charges.	
$	under $30
$$	$30–$50
$$$	$50–$75
$$$$	$75–$100
$$$$$	over $100

Left **1789** Right **Sequoia**

TOP 10 Places to Eat

1 Citronelle

Chef Michel Richard is famous for his innovative dishes. Described as French/Californian, the menu includes such items as Sonoma duck with succotash and *chateaubriand (see p63)*. *Latham Hotel, 3000 M St, NW • Map L2 • 202-625-2150 • Dis. access • $$$$$*

2 1789

Excellent American food. The elegant townhouse is divided into five themed rooms, and was popular with President Clinton *(see p63)*. Formal dress. *1226 36th St, NW • Map K2 • 202-965-1789 • $$$*

3 Sequoia

Famous for its beautiful views of the Potomac River, this is a haven for people-watching. The American cuisine, emphasizing seafood, enhances the setting. *3000 K St, NW • Map L3 • 202-944-4200 • Dis. access • $$$*

4 Zed's Ethiopian Cuisine

The large Ethiopian population in the city has produced a number of fine restaurants; this one is rated among the best. Delicious vegetarian dishes, as well as spicy meat and poultry. *1201 28th St, NW • Map L2 • 202-333-4710 • $$*

5 Clyde's of Georgetown

This long-time Georgetown favorite trucks in local produce and incorporates it into special menu items. *3236 M St, NW • Map L2 • 202-333-9180 • Dis. access • $$$*

6 Bread and Chocolate

A restaurant and bakery with great sandwiches, salads, soups, and desserts. No alcohol. *2301 M St, NW • Map M2 • 202-833-8360 • Dis. access • $*

7 Bistro Français

Unpretentious French dishes and a selection of wonderful pastries. *3124 M St, NW • Map L2 • 202-338-3830 • $$*

8 Mie n Yu

Crowds flock to this Asian fusion eatery for its festive atmosphere, funky menu, and fruity cocktails. *3125 M St, NW • Map L2 • 202-333-6122 • $$$*

9 Bangkok Joe's

Home-made dishes and pan-Asian delights burst with flavor at DC's only dumpling bar. *3000 K St, NW • Map L3 • 202-333-4422 • $$*

10 Miss Saigon

Vegetarian specials, as well as Vietnamese stir-fries, and curries. *3057 M St, NW • Map L2 • 202-333-5545 • Dis. access • $$*

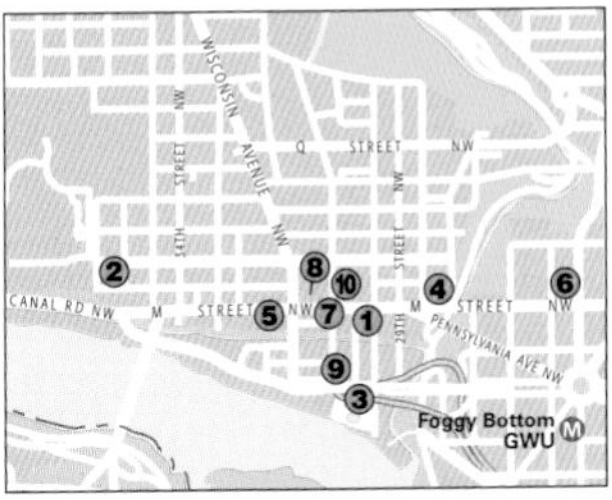

***Note:** Unless otherwise stated, all restaurants accept credit cards and serve vegetarian meals*

Left **Mount Vernon** Right **Bethesda**

Beyond the City Center

THE MONUMENTAL CORE OF WASHINGTON, DC *is so rich in sights that visitors may be tempted to look no farther. But many delights lie within easy reach of the city center. The Michigan Avenue NE area near North Capitol Street is home to the stunning Basilica of the National Shrine of the Immaculate Conception; the U Street NW corridor is a historic town center for the African-American community; Bethesda is filled with every kind of restaurant; the Southwest waterfront is busy with commercial fishing activity; while Old Town Alexandria has a beautifully restored downtown area and fine galleries.*

Washington National Cathedra

TOP 10 Sights

1. **Washington National Cathedral**
2. **Arlington Cemetery**
3. **Mount Vernon**
4. **Old Town Alexandria**
5. **Basilica of the National Shrine of the Immaculate Conception**
6. **U Street, NW**
7. **Southwest Waterfront**
8. **Bethesda, Maryland**
9. **Great Falls**
10. **National Air and Space Museum Steven F. Udvar-Hazy Center**

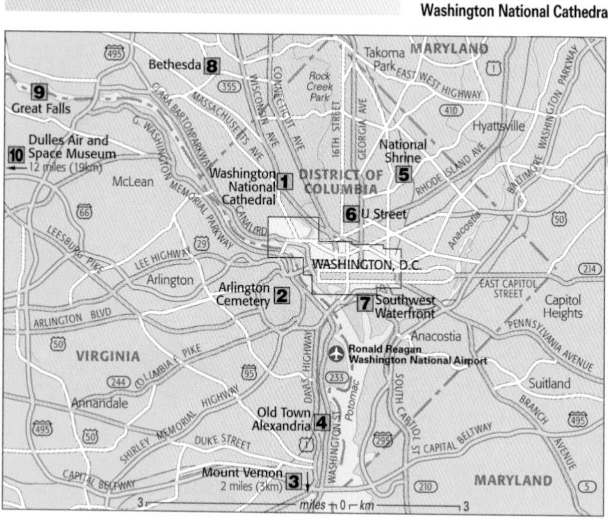

1 Washington National Cathedral

This noble hand-crafted church is so faultless that the cathedral seems to have belonged on its elevated site forever *(see pp26–7)*.

2 Arlington Cemetery

A visit to this solemn burial ground brings conflicting emotions – pride in the determination of defenders of freedom, pleasure in the presence of its great beauty, but dismay at the loss of so many lives marked by the arrays of headstones *(see pp30–31)*.

3 Mount Vernon

Without a doubt the finest current view of George Washington the man, and of the agrarian plantation life that was an important stream leading to the revolutionary break with Great Britain *(see pp32–5)*.

4 Old Town Alexandria

This lovely old city center, across the Potomac just beneath the capital, retains the charm and hospitality of its illustrious past while giving visitors all modern conveniences, including a metro station (King Street on the yellow and blue lines). Alexandria is noted for its historical and archeological museums, Gadsby's Tavern *(see p44)*, the evocative system of Civil War forts and defenses at Fort Ward, and its captivating residential architecture, civilized shops, and restaurants. *Map D5*

Lee-Fendall House Museum, Old Alexandria

Altar, Basilica of the National Shrine of the Immaculate Conception

5 Basilica of the National Shrine of the Immaculate Conception

This mammoth basilica, dedicated in 1959, incorporates more than 60 chapels and oratories that retell the diverse history of the Roman Catholic Church in the United States. Conceived in the grand style – it is the largest Roman Catholic church in the western hemisphere – the building combines Byzantine and Romanesque features, creating an intensely decorative but substantial effect. The interior is simply overwhelming in its grandeur, whatever your faith. There is also a cafeteria serving breakfast and lunch on the site, which is convenient because there are few nearby restaurants. Tours available. *400 Michigan Ave, NE • Map D3 • 202-526-8300 • Open Nov–Mar: 7am–6pm daily; Apr–Oct: 7am–7pm daily • Dis. access*

National Cathedral Schools

Like a medieval cathedral, National Cathedral is surrounded by some of the most prestigious prep schools in the city. St. Albans' alumni include Al Gore and Jesse Jackson, Jr. The all-girls National Cathedral School is alma mater to a number of Rockefellers and Roosevelts. Sidwell Friends School, just up Wisconsin Avenue, educated Chelsea Clinton, the Nixon daughters, Nancy Davis Reagan, and currently Barack Obama's daughters.

Duke Ellington Mural, U Street

6 U Street, NW

For much of the 20th century, U Street, NW was the main street of this bustling and prosperous African-American neighborhood. Opened as a movie theater in 1922, the Lincoln Theater *(see p59)* has now been refurbished and presents performances of every kind. Next door is the famous Ben's Chili Bowl, turning out great simple food for capacity crowds. The legendary jazz musician Duke Ellington *(see p47)* played his first paid performance at True Reformer Hall at the junction of 12th and U Street, NW. The poignant sculpture and plaza of the African-American Civil War Memorial *(see p49)* commemorates African-Americans who served in the Civil War. *Map N1*

7 Southwest Waterfront

This is a wonderful place for strolling, summer and winter. The diversity of Washington is on parade, the sailboats, yachts, and houseboats are picturesque, and the seafood – both cooked and raw – at the Southwest Fish Wharf is a showcase of what's best in eastern waters. The Fish Wharf is the current raucous embodiment of colorful markets that have flourished here continuously since about 1790. It is famed for its crabs, oysters, and clams, and also specializes in river fish not widely available elsewhere, such as perch and bass. *Water St, SW • Map D4*

8 Bethesda, Maryland

Locally, Bethesda is best known for its enormous quantity and range of restaurants, most of them clustered into a lively downtown area that still retains the atmosphere of a traditional town center. The high-end employment offered by Bethesda's world-renowned biotechnology industry, however, has also generated a spirited music, performance, and arts scene catering to its cultured and wealthy residents. The city is especially strong on public art. Its streets and parks spotlight distinguished contemporary works in every style, by way of sculpture and stunning painted murals. *Map C2*

Mural, Bethesda Avenue

Great Falls

9 Great Falls

About 15 miles (24 km) north of Washington, DC, the Potomac is rent by magnificent waterfalls over the crags and sluices of the eroded river bed. In the state of Virginia, Great Falls Park is reached from Old Dominion Drive (Route 738). It provides spectacular overlooks above the river, fine hiking trails, and the ruins of a small 19th-century town. On the Maryland side, the Great Falls area is part of the C&O Canal *(see p99)*. The Great Falls Tavern Visitor Center offers canal rides, hiking, and ranger-led tours and remarkable river views from the overlook on Olmstead Island. *Map A2 • Great Falls Tavern Visitor Center: 11710 MacArthur Blvd • 310-767-3714 • Open dawn–dusk daily*

10 National Air and Space Museum Steven F. Udvar-Hazy Center

This display and restoration center for some of the museum's magnificent collection of historic aviation and space artifacts *(see pp16–17)* opened in December 2003 near Dulles International Airport. Two giant hangars with accompanying support buildings provide over 760,000 sq ft (70,611 sq m) of much-needed extra display space. *South of main terminal at Dulles International Airport, near intersection of rtes 28 & 50*

A Day in Old Town Alexandria

Morning

Begin at Christ Church *(118 N Washington St • Open 9am–4pm Mon–Sat, 2–4pm Sun • Donation)*, a handsome Georgian-style building completed in 1773. George Washington's box pew has been preserved. Then turn right onto Cameron Street toward the harbor. Continue three blocks and turn right onto North Royal Street. The two buildings on your right comprise **Gadsby's Tavern Museum** *(see p44)*. The half-hour tours are a fascinating introduction to colonial life in the city.

Head back to the harbor, turn left just before the Chart House Restaurant, and continue a half block to the Torpedo Factory Food Pavilion, with its Italian and Oriental specialties, and coffee bar. Take-out food can be eaten on the Pavilion's deck with its river views, or, a few steps upriver, in the lush Founder's Park.

Afternoon

Heading out of the Food Pavilion, directly ahead is the ticket booth for the Potomac Riverboat Company, which operates the *Admiral Tilp*. It provides a narrated 40-minute tour of the waterfront and nearby points of interest.

To the right of the tour boat kiosk is the **Torpedo Factory** *(see p112)*. It takes at least an hour for even a quick inspection of the studios of the over 165 artists here, so take a leisurely late afternoon deciding which piece you'd like to take home.

Following pages: **Mural in Anacostia**

Left **Capitol Coin and Stamp** Right **Logo, Torpedo Factory Art Center**

TOP 10 Shops

1 Chocolate Moose
This novelty gift shop stocks quality, eclectic items, including jewelry, housewares, toys and confections. Bright papers and gift bags ensure you won't return home without a well-wrapped souvenir. *1743 L St, NW • Map N3*

2 Old Print Gallery
The gallery presents a huge collection of fine art prints arranged by themes. An outstanding source for political cartoons, city views, sporting prints, and historical subjects. *1220 31st St, NW • Map L2*

3 Politics and Prose
A bookstore with a large selection of works on politics, culture, and government. A cheerful place, despite its serious selection, with a coffee bar. *5015 Connecticut Ave, NW • Map H2*

4 Capitol Coin and Stamp
The shop has a variety of political memorabilia with a huge price range. For non-specialists, the colorful political campaign stamps, buttons, and posters will be of interest. *1001 Connecticut Ave, NW • Map N3*

5 Tysons Corner Center and Galleria At Tysons II
Buses run from Ballston Metro to this huge shopping site. Caters to every pocket, from Gap to designer labels. A pleasant place to spend the day – with cinemas and restaurants *(see p57)*.

6 Torpedo Factory Art Center
The building was originally a factory to manufacture torpedoes. Today, the site contains 82 studios and six galleries where artists and craftspeople create work and offer it for sale on site. Prints, ceramics, photography, painting, and sculpture. *105 N Union St, Alexandria • Map D5*

7 Kramerbooks
This Dupont Circle landmark has a fantastic collection of books and a knowledgeable staff. There's also a bar and restaurant (Afterwords Cafe). Open 24 hours on Fridays and Saturdays. *1517 Connecticut Ave, NW • Map N2*

8 Sullivan's Toy Store
An astounding range of playthings can be found in this store. The real stars are the items with a link to the past: model kits, craft supplies, board games, and kites. *3412 Wisconsin Ave, NW • Map G4*

9 Copenhaver
Appreciating the formalities of communication, Copenhaver sells the tools for it: elegant writing paper, envelopes, and pens. *1301 Connecticut Ave, NW • Map N2*

10 Kron Chocolatier
This store is famous for its molded chocolate items – bears, sports cars, even the US Capitol. They also sell greeting cards made of chocolate. *Mazza Galleria, 5300 Wisconsin Ave, NW • Map G2*

Browse the Torpedo Factory website at www.torpedofactory.org for their unique arts and crafts

Price Categories

For a three-course meal for one with half a bottle of wine (or equivalent meal), taxes and extra charges.	**$** under $30 **$$** $30–$50 **$$$** $50–$75 **$$$$** $75–$100 **$$$$$** over $100

Left **Green Papaya** Right **Two Amys**

Top 10 Places to Eat

1 Two Amys
Within walking distance of the National Cathedral, this is Washington locals' favorite pizzeria – expect to wait for a table during peak times. Authentic Neapolitan pizzas baked in a wood-burning oven. *3715 Macomb St, NW • Map H4 • 202-885-5700 • Dis. access • $*

2 American Tap Room
This modern version of the traditional American tap room offers an inviting atmosphere, a large selection of beers, and a classic grill menu. Brunch, lunch, and dinner. *7278 Woodmont Ave, Bethesda, MD • Map C2 • 301-656-1366 • Dis. access • $$*

3 Bacchus Restaurant
The *mezze* at this Lebanese restaurant are delicious. Marinated chicken, eggplant, hummus, and squid fill numerous little dishes with flavor. *7945 Norfolk Ave, Bethesda, MD • Map C2 • 301-657-1722 • Dis. access • $$*

4 Passage to India
The Indian menu here does not limit itself to any particular region of India. The *daal* and butter chicken are rich and smooth. *4931 Cordell Ave, Bethesda, MD • Map C2 • 301-656-3373 • $$*

5 Grand Cru
This tiny café has an exquisite menu, including succulent *filet mignon* and moreish *crème brûlée*. Doubling as a wine shop, its choice is outstanding. Dine in the courtyard in good weather. *4401 Wilson Blvd, Arlington, VA • Map C4 • 703-243-7900 • $$$*

6 Green Papaya
At this Vietnamese restaurant, lemongrass beef and chicken are popular. *4922 Elm St, Bethesda, MD • Map C2 • 301-654-8241 • $$*

7 Bilbo Baggins Restaurant
The menu fuses dishes from around the world and features a wonderful selection of beers. *208 Queen St, Alexandria, VA • Map D5 • 703-683-0300 • Dis. access • $*

8 Jackie's Restaurant
Housed in a redesigned auto parts garage, Jackie's adds a touch of fun to eating out. Enjoy a modern American menu including free-range meats, organic produce, and seafood. *8081 Georgia Ave, Silver Spring, MD • Map D2 • 301-565-9700 • $$$*

9 Restaurant Eve
Wood and amber create a cozy ambience here. There is a cocktails and nibbles lounge, a bistro, as well as a tasting room. Don't miss the butter-poached Maine lobster. *110 S. Pitt St, Alexandria • Map D5 • 703-706-0450 • $$$$*

10 Taverna Cretekou
Fantastic Greek food, ouzo, and traditional dancing can be found at this popular restaurant. *818 King St, Alexandria, VA • Map D5 • 703-548-8688 • $$*

Note: *Unless otherwise stated, all restaurants accept credit cards and serve vegetarian meals*

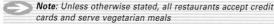

STREETSMART

Left **Greyhound bus** Right **Amtrak reception desk**

Top 10 Getting to Washington, DC

1 By Air from North America

Three airports serve Washington – Reagan Washington National, Dulles International, and Baltimore/Washington International. Twenty-four US, Canadian, and regional airlines have flights to one or more of these. For downtown Washington, Reagan is the airport of choice. *Reagan National (DCA): 703-417-8000, www.mwaa.com • Dulles International (IAD): 703-572-2700, www.mwaa.com • Baltimore/Washington International (BWI): 800-I-FLY-BWI, www.bwiairport.com*

2 By Air from Europe

Most major European airlines serve Dulles, either direct or by changing planes in New York or Boston. These include British Airways, Air France, Aer Lingus, KLM, Lufthansa, SAS, and Virgin. British Airways also serves BWI.

3 By Air from Australasia

Air Canada provides a service via Halifax to Sydney; Qantas and American Airlines fly via Los Angeles. Connections are available from any of the DC airports.

4 By Air from Central and South America

Grupo Taca has flights between more than 40 cities in 19 countries in North, Central, and South America. United and American Airlines have routes between Washington and Central and South America, via Miami.

5 Ronald Reagan Washington National Airport

The layout of this airport is a long walkway with a semicircular bend at the end – use the shuttle bus that stops at marked locations. A Metrorail stop is right outside the northern terminals. Taxi service from the airport to the National Mall is about 15 minutes and costs around $20. The SuperShuttle provides transit from door to door.

6 Dulles International Airport

The terminal consists of a main building and two midfield concourses reached by shuttles. There is no metro stop, but the Washington Flyer coach provides transportation to the West Falls Church Metrorail station. One-way taxi fares to the city are about $50, but shuttle transportation to many hotels can be arranged from the terminal. The airport is 26 miles (42 km) from Washington.

7 BWI Thurgood Marshall International Airport

There are five concourses in this airport. A BWI Express Metrobus provides transportation to and from the Greenbelt Metro station. BWI also has its own rail station with direct trains to Union Station. Taxis to the city cost about $60. The terminal is 30 miles (48 km) from Washington.

8 By Train

Amtrak provides intercity rail transportation to Washington. The Acela Express is the quickest way to travel. Amtrak has a reduced-fare USA Rail Pass, which is worth considering if traveling widely across the country. Union Station *(see p71)* is the main terminal. *Amtrak: 800-USA-RAIL/800-872-7245; www.amtrak.com*

9 By Car

Washington has the second worst congestion in the country, which makes driving a less attractive way to get to the city, but larger hotels have parking (about $20 per day), and garages are available. Driving routes to D.C. are I-95 and I-270 from the north, I-66 from the west, I-95 and I-395 from the south, and US 50 from the east.

10 By Bus

The main bus terminals are behind Union Station. Greyhound Lines connect with more than 3,700 locations, and offer low-cost passes for easy travel. Other bus lines arrive and depart across the street. *Greyhound: 800-231-2222*

Foreign nationals traveling on a visa are registered on arrival – fingerprints, personal details, and photos are taken.

Left **Metrorail sign** Center **Taxi** Right **Road sign**

TOP 10 Getting Around Washington, DC

1 Metrorail
For most destinations in the city, Metrorail, the subway-surface rail system, is the best way to get around. Service is frequent, cars are clean and comfortable, stops are convenient to major sights, and the system is among the safest in the world. Fares depend on distance traveled, from $1.95 to $5.00. There are 1-day, 7-day, and 28-day passes that allow unlimited trips for a reduced fare. ✆ *Metrorail: www.wmata.com • Info: 202-637-7000; 6am–8:30pm Mon–Fri, 7am–8:30pm Sat & Sun*

2 Metrobus and the Circulator
The public bus system serves all areas of the city, including destinations not served by Metrorail. Exact change is required (regular routes are $1.50). The Circulator bus travels between Georgetown and Union Station from the Convention Center to Southwest and back every 5–10 mins from 7am–9pm daily. Exact change is required ($1.70 fare). It is worth buying a SmarTrip card for discounts on metro and bus travel – as well as for free bus-to-bus transfers. ✆ *301-925-7957; www.dccirculator.com*

3 Tour Bus Lines
The Old Town Trolley runs a National Mall/ Downtown loop, National Cathedral loop and an Arlington Cemetery loop. See floodlit memorials on the trolley's popular "Monuments by Moonlight" tour. Passengers can disembark and reboard at any stop. A similar service is offered by Open Top Sightseeing. ✆ *Old Town Trolley: www.oldtowntrolley.com • www.opentopsightseeing.com, 1877-332-8689*

4 Taxis
Taxis in DC are metered. Expect to pay a "drop" fee of $3.00, and 25 cents every one sixth of a mile. Luggage and additional passengers are extra. The maximum fare within the district is $19.00.

5 Walking
Washington is a city built for walking: sidewalks are wide, intersections have pedestrian walk signs, and drivers are courteous. But scale can be misleading, so wear comfortable shoes.

6 Car Sharing
Zipcar (www.zipcar.com) is an hourly car rental program. Plan members ($50 annual membership fee) can reserve a car, pick it up at the Metro station nearest their destination, then return it. Rates start at $7 (gas and insurance included).

7 Rental Cars
Rental car companies are located at all airports, Union Station, and many other locations. You can find the nearest one with the help of the *Yellow Pages*. Renting a car requires a valid driver's license and a major credit card. Drivers must be at least 25 years old. Most cars are automatic, but some companies offer stick-shift controls but such a request has to be made in advance. ✆ *Avis: www.avis.com, 800-230-4898 • Budget: www.budgetrentacar.com, 800-527-0700 • Hertz: www.hertz.com, 800-654-3131*

8 Parking
Parking at a car lot will cost about $20 per day and about $12 for two hours. Street parking meters have a two-hour maximum, and fines are high. Parking is prohibited on many downtown streets during rush hour, with hours posted on curbside signs. Your car will be towed if you disregard them.

9 Excursions
Some out-of-town attractions such as Mount Vernon *(see pp32–5)* can be reached by tour bus lines. Others are also served by rail. Most out-of-town destinations have ample parking.

10 Maps
The Smithsonian Information Center has brochures and maps; hotels and newsstands usually sell maps of the metropolitan area and the rail and bus system.

Left **Visitor Center** Right **Metrobus**

Top 10 Sources of Information

1 Washington DC Chamber of Commerce

The center for both tourist and business travel to Washington, the organization has an outstanding website and provides information by mail. The site has search capabilities for hotels, shops, restaurants, tourist sights, and transportation. *1213 K St, NW • Map P3 • www.dcchamber.org • 202-638-7330 • Open 9am–4:30pm Mon–Fri (closed Sat & Sun)*

2 Washington DC Visitor Information Center

Advertised as "one-stop shopping" for visitor information, this center comes close to meeting its claim. The center gives advice to walk-in visitors, makes hotel reservations with special discounts, and provides information on tourist sights. *1300 Pennsylvania Ave, NW, Ronald Reagan Building and International Trade Center • Map P4 • www.vrc.dc.gov • 202-289-8317 • Summer: open 8:30am–5:30pm Mon-Fri, 9am–4pm Sat (closed Sun); Winter: open 9am–4:30pm Mon–Fri (closed Sat & Sun)*

3 Metrorail & Circulator Bus

Hotels generally have metro information and maps, but the Metrorail's website is also excellent *(see p117)*, and system information is displayed in all stations and stops.

4 Smithsonian Institution Information Center

Before you arrive in Washington, the Smithsonian's website is the most convenient source of information. Once in the city, anyone heading for Smithsonian museums or the zoo should visit the Smithsonian Information Center, which also provides interesting displays of its own. *1000 Jefferson Drive, SW • Map Q5 • www.si.edu • 202-631-1000 • Open 9am–5:30pm daily*

5 National Park Service

Many of the sites on the National Mall, especially monuments and memorials, are the responsibility of the National Park Service. Park Service employees will be able to answer most questions. *900 Ohio Drive, SW • Map P6 • www.nps.gov • 202-426-6841*

6 Washington Post

This internationally respected newspaper is an institution in DC. As well as news and politics, it is indispensable for its coverage of what's going on in the entertainment and cultural worlds of the city. In its Friday Weekend tabloid, nearly everything that is current is listed. The *Post's* website (www.washingtonpost.com) is almost as good.

7 Washington City Paper

The *City Paper*'s readers are devoted to its coverage of the local music scene and its irreverent look at local culture. Issued each Thursday, it is available free at newsstands, bars and restaurants. *www.washingtoncitypaper.com*

8 Washingtonian Magazine

A city lifestyle magazine, *Washingtonian* provides listings and commentary on cultural institutions and events. It is well known for its coverage of restaurants, featuring the "100 Best." Its website (www.washingtonian.com) has a listing of "100 Cheap Eats."

9 International and Domestic Arrivals Desk for Travelers

At Dulles International Airport *(see p116)*, foreign language assistance is available on the lower level at the west and east ends of the concourse near international arrivals. *703-572-2536/2537 (international); 703-572-8296/8297 (domestic)*

10 Travelers' Aid Society

Travelers' Aid is located at airports and in Union Station *(see p71)* near McDonald's. It provides free advice to anyone stranded in the city and needing directions. *Union Station • 202-371-1937 • info@travelersaid.org*

Left **Traffic jam** Right **Reading a street map**

Top 10 Things to Avoid

1 Security Delays and Exclusions
Following the 2001 terrorist attacks on the United States, security precautions have been strengthened. Visitors need a government-issued photo ID to enter most government buildings, some office buildings, and even some nightclubs. Visitors to public buildings, including the Smithsonian museums, are prohibited from carrying aerosol and non-aerosol sprays, cans and bottles, food, knives of any sort or other sharp objects such as razors or box-cutters, and mace or pepper spray. Large backpacks are also not allowed, and handbags and briefcases will be searched. People have been delayed or even arrested for remarks officials consider "inappropriate," so don't crack jokes about bombs or weapons. If traveling under the visa-waiver scheme, register and pay online at https://esta.cbp.dhs.gov 72 hours before.

2 Exhaustion
The openness of the Mall can make distances look shorter than they are. If you start at the Smithsonian Metro station, walk to the Lincoln Memorial, to the Capitol, and back to the Metro stop, you will have covered 5 miles (8 km). Whether in DC's humid summer or windy winter, that can be a tiring hike, especially for children.

3 Misinterpreting Washington's Quadrants
The city plan of DC arranges all addresses within four quadrants, centered on the dome of the Capitol. Numbered (north-south) and lettered (east-west) streets start on each side of the Capitol. There is a 1st St east of the Capitol and a completely different 1st St west of it. An E St lies north of the Capitol and a different E St south of it. To locate an address, the extension NW, NE, SE, or SW must be noted.

4 Bad Weather
In July and August, temperatures range from about 85°F (30°C) to 95°F (35°C), but the real problem can be humidity. Walk slowly and drink lots of fluids – or visit at some other time of the year. Winters, especially January and February, can be windy and raw. Snow and ice storms produce beautiful scenery around the monuments and gardens, but they can paralyze the city temporarily.

5 Street Crime
The greatest protection from street crime is alertness. Thieves depend largely on surprise. Don't carry large amounts of cash or valuables. Keep an accurate record of what's in your wallet, including card numbers and phone numbers of credit card issuers.

6 Dangerous Areas
Tourist zones are safe day and night, but if you want to go to a destination outside these areas, especially at night, ask at your hotel desk for their recommendation.

7 Traffic Jams
Traffic congestion can interfere with plans. Traffic moves erratically and slowly, and getting into and out of the city in rush hour (about 6:30–9:30am and 4–7pm) may incur delays of 45 minutes or more.

8 Discarding Metro Farecard
Metrorail uses a farecard system in which the turnstiles deduct the cost of your trip as you leave the station. You use the same farecard both to enter and to leave, so don't throw it away after getting on the train.

9 Car Break-ins
No matter where you park, don't leave anything in the passenger compartment. If your car radio, GPS, or CD player is removable, take it with you.

10 Escalator Etiquette
Washington has countless escalators, some of them among the longest in the world. Washingtonians can become angry when the way is blocked – you should stand single-file and to the right, or walk on the left.

Left **Union Station shopping mall** Right **Georgetown shops**

Top 10 Shopping Tips

1 Mall Shopping

If there's one shopping area convenient to Downtown to head for, it would have to be the Fashion Centre at Pentagon City *(see p56)*. The high-quality, high-service Nordstrom's is the anchor store, accompanied by Macy's and over 150 other stores. Tysons Corner *(see p57)* is a gigantic complex of two enclosed malls with a huge number and variety of stores and is the most popular shopping destination in the area. Take the Metro Blue or Yellow Line to Pentagon City. Buses to Tysons leave from Ballston Metro.

2 Georgetown

This has long been an outstanding area for antiques, fashion, and the unique and unusual *(see p57)*. If you plan to visit Georgetown for shopping, taxi is the best way to get there; the Georgetown Metro connection *(see p100)* provides a shuttle from the nearest Metrorail stations, and the Circulator bus runs from many stops in the city center *(see p117)*.

3 Seasonal Sales and Promotions

No-sales-tax weeks are popular in Washington. Usually two or three weeks before Christmas, these events shave extra percentage points off prices that are often already reduced. Black Friday, the day after Thanksgiving, offers big discounts. Post-Christmas clearances are also magnets for shoppers. Promotions are common for Presidents' Day in February, July 4th, back-to-school in late August, Columbus Day in October, and Veterans' Day in November.

4 Newspaper Specials

Retailers from small shops to huge department stores have sales on special merchandise, overstocks, and regular products to attract customers. The newspapers are the way to find these savings, such as the *Washington Post (see p118)* and the *Washington Times*. Sunday editions, in particular, contain many coupons.

5 Sales Tax

The sales tax on general merchandise in Washington is currently 5.75 percent (10 percent for food/beverages). In Virginia jurisdictions, it is 5 percent, and in Maryland it is 6 percent.

6 Shopping Hours

Mall and chain stores are usually open from 10am to 9pm Monday to Saturday and noon to 6pm on Sunday. Downtown and independent shops operate 10am to 6pm Monday to Saturday. Most shops in Georgetown stay open until 9pm.

7 Museum Shops

The museum shops *(see p83)* have merchandise at all prices. Items costing less than a dollar are lined up next to others costing several hundred dollars or more. Much of the stock in the better museum shops can be purchased nowhere else, so they are well worth a visit.

8 Street Vendors

These have thinned on Washington streets as a result of heightened government security. Interesting, cheap T-shirts are still available, however, along with other souvenir clothing and food.

9 Yard Sales

Private garage and yard sales are held throughout the city, usually on Saturday or Sunday mornings beginning at 8–9am, and bargains are still to be found. Find listings in the *Washington Post* and the *Washington City Paper (see p118)* or the many online classified advertising sites.

10 Senior Discounts

These popular senior discount shopping days at local department stores are less common than they once were, but they still exist. If you are shopping at a mall or large chain or department store, ask at the information or customer service desk.

The best website for finding current yard sales in the city is www.washingtoncitypaper.com

Left **Washington taxi** Center & Right **Washington bars**

TOP 10 Eating and Drinking Tips

1 Alcohol Age Limits

In Washington and surrounding jurisdictions, the legal age for purchasing or drinking alcoholic beverages is 21. The law is strictly enforced. You will need a photo ID regardless of your age. Many clubs and other venues allow under-21 patrons to enter and enjoy the show, but without a wristband or stamped marking, they are not allowed to buy alcohol. It is becoming common for clubs and rock concert venues to require photo ID from everyone, no matter what their age is.

2 Sales Tax

Tax on restaurant food and on food for immediate consumption is 10 percent. Diners with budget concerns should take this into account, along with tips. A $20 meal with tax and tip actually costs almost $26.

3 Getting Home

The metro closes at midnight during the week and at 3am on Saturday and Sunday mornings, but many clubs, bars, and restaurants stay open later. In most areas there should be no problem finding a taxi on the street. Failing that, you can telephone for a taxi, but there is a surcharge. If your hotel is in the suburbs, the taxi fare can be expensive.

4 Microbreweries

Washington is a good place to enjoy unconventional and microbrewed beer. Capitol City Brewing Company has a number of locations in the area. The District Chop House and Brewery has its own award-winning brewer and serves a variety of ales to complement the food. The Church Key has over 500 types of beer including some rare labels. *Capitol City Brewing Company: 2 Massachusetts Ave, NE • District Chop House and Brewery: 509 7th St, NW • Church Key: 1337 14th St, NW, 2nd floor*

5 Tipping

Restaurant checks rarely include a charge for service. In most restaurants, leaving 18 percent of the total charge is common practice. In addition, tax will be added to your bill. Customers at a bar may leave 10–15 percent of the bar bill or $1 per drink. In a few of the finest restaurants, it is appropriate to tip the *maître d'* $5 or more if he or she stage-manages the service at your table.

6 Cell Phones

At most restaurants in the city, it is usually considered bad manners to leave cell phones turned on or to carry on phone conversations inside the restaurant while dining.

7 Smoking

Smoking is banned in all public buildings, including bars and restaurants. Cigarettes can be purchased by those over 18 years old; do remember that proof of age is required, so carry a photo ID.

8 Farmers' Markets

For carry-around food and drink, think farmers' markets. These are popular features and often have locally grown fresh produce and other products. There's a year-round Saturday and Sunday market at Eastern Market *(see p74)* and an April to December seasonal market on Sunday morning at Dupont Circle.

9 Tasting Events

With its embassies, government affairs, and high-powered dinner parties, Washington is a big wine and food city. There are tastings and cooking demonstrations or classes almost every day. *Washingtonian Magazine (see p118)* keeps an up-to-date registry on its website.

10 Children

If you're traveling with kids and want an all-child-friendly row of easy-to-deal-with restaurants, you can't go wrong in the block of storefronts across from the National Zoo on Connecticut Avenue *(see pp28–9)*.

For current information on tastings visit the website www.washingtonian.com

Left **TicketPlace discount ticket booth** Right **Takeout food outlet**

TOP 10 Tips for Budget Travelers

1 Camping

While there are no campsites or RV campgrounds within the District of Columbia, nearby sites are practical. Cherry Hill Park is served by a municipal bus hourly and Grayline bus three times daily and is just 3 miles (5 km) from the Greenbelt Metro stop. Capitol KOA runs free shuttle buses to the Metro. *Cherry Hill Park: 9800 Cherry Hill Rd, College Park, MD; www.cherryhillpark.com; 301-937-7116 • Capitol KOA Campground: 768 Cecil Ave, N, Millersville, MD; www.capitolKOA.com; 410-923-2771 or 800-562-0248*

2 Discount Tickets

TicketPlace sells half-price theater tickets. Tickets available in advance and on the day of the performance. It is also a Ticketmaster outlet, so regular reservations can be made here. *TicketPlace: 407 7th St, NW • Map Q4 • 202-TICKETS • www.ticketplace.org • Closed Thanksgiving, Dec 25, Jan 1 • Open 11am–6pm Wed–Fri, 10am–5pm Sat, noon–4pm Sun*

3 Low Season

Discount hotel rates become available during the summer, when the Congress is closed, and in the last two weeks in December, and early January. Many hotels offer weekend packages. April through June is the most expensive time.

4 Hotel Discounts

When making reservations, ask if any discounts are available. Many hotels provide discounts for AAA (American Automobile Association) and AARP (American Association of Retired Persons). The Visitors' Center *(see p118)* can book rooms at a discount. The best rates can be found on the Internet.

5 Travel Agents

One resource for finding lower airfares is often neglected today: an experienced travel agent. Fares contracted through a reputable travel agency are almost always lower than those offered by airlines. Similarly, online air reservations can save money. Expedia (www.expedia.com), Travelocity (www.travelocity.com), and Orbitz (www.orbitz.com) are the most popular.

6 Takeout Food

Many smaller hotels that do not have room service or a full-time restaurant will allow patrons to order takeout, delivered to the hotel.

7 Picnics

Delis and produce stores serve every neighborhood. Picnics require finesse in high-security times: if you plan to visit museums or government buildings, you can't carry a knife. Think bite-size items such as cherry tomatoes and pre-cut cheese, and buy drinks on site. You also can't take food inside, so plan an outdoor spot.

8 Free Entertainment

Take advantage of free entertainment whenever you can, such as the film and concert series at the Library of Congress *(see pp24–5)*. The Millennium Stage at the Kennedy Center *(see p91)* has a great free performance every day. The National Gallery of Art *(see pp20–23)* also has a concert series, and the Hirshhorn Museum *(see p77)* shows movies.

9 Cheap Menus

You won't find the traditional $3.99 meatloaf dinner in Washington anymore, but *Washingtonian Magazine*'s "Cheap Eats" list is a great starting point for affordable food in pleasant surroundings. DC's Restaurant Week runs twice a year with discounted three-course meals (spring and fall) *(see p118)*.

10 Hostels

There is only one hostel in the city, and it is, not surprisingly, in very great demand. Reservations are essential, made as far in advance as possible. *Hostelling International Washington, DC: 1009 11th Street, NW • Map P3 • 202-737-2333 • www.hiwashingtondc.org*

Left **Tourmobile bus** Right **Shopping mall**

TOP 10 Tips for Disabled Travelers

1 Metrorail
The Metro is fully accessible to disabled travelers. The website *(see p117)* gives detailed information about accessibility and has a link for out-of-town visitors who will be using the system temporarily. Tactile maps for the system are available at the Columbia Lighthouse for the Blind. Over 70 percent of Metrobus equipment consists of kneeling buses or buses with lifts. *Columbia Lighthouse for the Blind: 202-454-6400 • www.clb.org*

2 Old Town Trolley
This bus service *(see p117)* provides access to mobility-restricted passengers, who can transfer from their wheelchairs to priority seating. Wheelchair storage is available. For convenience, book at least 24 hours in advance. Passengers who need a chair lift can request one at any stop, and a vehicle will be dispatched.

3 Government Buildings
Most have good access for the disabled, but require advance notice for special services such as signed tours. In some instances, accessibility has been lessened due to heightened security measures. The information numbers *(see p118)* will have current accessibility conditions.

4 Shopping Malls
Most of the larger shopping malls are easily accessible, and all have disabled facilities. Union Station *(see p71)* is notable because it has a metro stop in the building. Other accessible shopping areas in the city limits include the Old Post Office Pavilion, Georgetown Park Mall, and The Shops at National Place *(see pp56–7)*.

5 Access Information Inc
This company publishes the *Access Entertainment Guide* for the Washington, D.C. area. Its website provides reviews of many business and tourist attractions from the point of view of disabled access. It also covers airports, hotels, museums, arenas and concert venues, shops, cinemas, and transportation. *Access Information Inc: 21618 Slidell Road, Boyds, MD • www.disabilityguide.org • 301-528-8664*

6 Hotels
Nearly all major hotels have some rooms that are wheelchair-accessible. Some have roll-in showers. Other services, such as flashing-light fire alarms, tactile paging, or door-knockers, are widely but not universally available. Information can best be obtained by calling a hotel directly.

7 FDR Memorial
Many places in Washington are welcoming to people with disabilities, but probably none more so than the FDR Memorial *(see p82)*. All four outdoor rooms of this monument are completely accessible. Inscriptions are given in Braille. A sculpture of Franklin D. Roosevelt in his wheelchair has been added to the memorial.

8 National Zoological Park
Washington's Zoo *(see pp28–9)* has disabled access to nearly all its public areas. The panda environment, for example, is designed with ramps, and viewing angles are calculated to suit the mobility-impaired. Visitors in manual wheelchairs should be warned that the grades on some of the paths are steep.

9 Service Animals
These are allowed anywhere the general public is admitted. It can be convenient to have special harnesses, but these are not required.

10 Smithsonian Information
"Smithsonian Access" is online (www.si.edu/visit/visitors_with_disabilities.hfm) and is also available in large-print, audiocassette, Braille, and computer disk at Smithsonian Information *(see p118)*.

All Metro stations are equipped with elevators, when out of service a shuttle service is provided upon request.

Left **ATM machine** Right **Credit cards**

TOP 10 Banking and Communications

1 ATM Machines

ATM machines are found everywhere in the city, including the majority of major sights. Cirrus, Plus, and NCYE are the most common networks. Use ATMs to withdraw money during the day in well-populated areas, minimizing the risk of robbery. An administration fee of $2–3 may be charged by most banks.

2 Banks

You can be almost certain that all banks will be open 9am–2pm Monday to Friday and 9am–noon on Saturday except federal holidays. Some branches have extended hours. Most banks in tourist areas will have services for travelers, including redeeming travelers' checks and currency exchange.

3 Credit Cards

A credit card is essential for car rentals *(see p117)*. Bank debit cards are not accepted for this purpose. Nearly all tourist-related businesses and institutions accept credit cards. It is a good idea to keep a record of the telephone number for reporting credit card thefts.

4 Travelers' Checks

Travelers' checks in US dollars are accepted the same as cash almost everywhere. Restaurants, stores, and tourist sites usually don't even ask for identification, although banks will often ask for a photo ID. Travelers' checks in foreign currencies can be cashed and exchanged at some, but not all, banks or major hotels, with a valid passport. Keep the proof of purchase separate from the checks.

5 Telephones

The Washington, DC area code is 202. Nearby Virginia is 703; Maryland is 240, 301 and 410. Directory assistance from most phones is reached by dialing 411. Cell and wireless coverage is excellent in the immediate area. Using the telephone in your hotel room is the most expensive way to make calls.

6 US Postal Service

Union Station *(see p71)* and all three airports *(see p116)* provide postal services for travelers. Blue postal drop boxes are located all over the city. Stamps can be purchased at many hotels, museum and tourist-site gift shops, larger grocery stores, and, of course, post offices. You can find the post office nearest you on the Postal Service website or from their toll-free number. *US Postal Service: www.usps.com, 800-275-8777*

7 UPS and Federal Express

Many tourists like to mail home gifts they have bought rather than tote them in baggage. The Postal Service can be used for this, but United Parcel Service (UPS) and Federal Express have more convenient drop-off locations. It is possible to arrange pickup at most hotels. *UPS: www.ups.com, 800-742-5877 • Federal Express: www.fedex.com, 1-800-463-3339*

8 Internet and Fax

Washington and the surrounding areas are thoroughly wired for Internet connection. Most major hotels have fax facilities and provision for connecting to the Internet, either in-room or in a business center. As well as Internet cafés, most general cafés and coffee shops will have Wi-Fi access.

9 Currency

The US currency is the dollar, and one dollar is made up of 100 cents. Visitors from outside the US should become familiar with the currency in advance. The counterfeit-proof bills can be difficult to distinguish from each other.

10 Currency Exchange

Exchange a small amount of currency at the airport and then convert more as needed at city banks where rates are better. Most legal currencies can be exchanged somewhere in Washington.

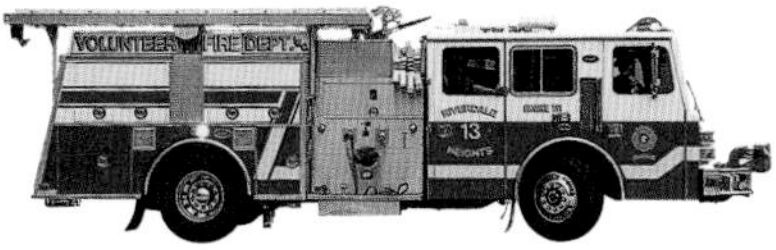

Left **Police Badge** Center **Fire engine** Right **Hospital Sign**

TOP 10 Security and Health

1 Emergency Numbers

Anywhere in or near the city, dialing 911 will summon police, fire, and rescue personnel and equipment as needed. The local 911 system has caller-ID and is able to automatically identify the address from which a call is placed. But this doesn't work as effectively from a cell or wireless phone, so look around for landmarks before you call. To contact the police for a non-emergency dial 311. You can reach Metro transit police at 202-962-2121.

2 Pharmacies

The CVS drugstore chain has 24-hour pharmacies at Dupont Circle, 2240 M St, NW, 1199 Vermont Ave, NW, and 4555 Wisconsin Ave, NW. These can refer you to pharmacies in other areas.

3 Hospitals and Dentists

Georgetown University Hospital provides a free physician referral service from 9am to 5pm, Monday to Friday. The District of Columbia Dental Society operates a free dental telephone referral service, 8am to 4pm. Most hotels can make physician and dental referrals.

Georgetown University Hospital: 3800 Reservoir Rd NW, Map K2, 202-342-2400 (doctor's referral) • D.C. Dental Society: 202-547-7613

4 Ambulances

An ambulance can be dispatched to emergency health situations by calling 911. Hospital emergency rooms, if you are nearby, are a possible alternative in a crisis, but ambulance crews start stabilizing treatment immediately.

5 Heat Exhaustion

This is a real possibility in summer. Wear light clothing, set a leisurely pace, stay in the shade when possible, and drink plenty of fluids. If you feel fatigued, light-headed, or weak, drink something and sit in a cool place. If you don't feel better soon, get medical attention – acute heat exhaustion can be life-threatening.

6 Driving

Drivers and passengers, front and back, are required to wear seat belts. Children eight years old and under must be seated in a child-restraint seat. Laws against drinking and driving are strictly enforced by the police.

7 Pedestrian Crossings

Washington drivers are not as hazardous as those in some cities. The biggest exception is running red lights. Make certain that opposing traffic has stopped before venturing onto the crosswalk. Be aware that it is legal to turn right at a red light, even when pedestrians have a green "walk" light.

8 Escalators

Washington is a city of escalators, and there have been a surprising number of deaths and injuries. Use the handrail, stand to the right, and keep loose clothing and shoelaces away from moving parts at the sides and bottom and top of the escalator. Use an elevator if you have children in a stroller or are carrying heavy luggage.

9 Metrorail

The system can be very crowded during rush hour. Especially if you are traveling with children, be certain to keep your party together. Locals generally have a plan for what to do if a child ends up on the train and the parents don't, or vice versa. The usual drill is for the child to get off the train at the next stop and wait for the parents to arrive. If it's the child that doesn't get on, he or she waits for the parents to backtrack to the station.

10 Boating

A number of rental services provide equipment for boating on the Potomac. This can be great fun, but the Potomac is dangerous. Follow all safety rules, and be certain to use the safety vests provided. The Great Falls area *(see p109)* is extremely hazardous. People die every year after falling from the rocks here.

Left **Willard Inter-Continental** Right **Jefferson Hotel**

Top 10 Historic Hotels

1 Willard Inter-Continental

This is certainly among the most historic of hotels. Epochal events, including the birth of the League of Nations, were discussed here by principal figures. Royalty from all over the world have been guests *(see p88).* *1401 Pennsylvania Ave, NW • Map P4 • 202-628-9100 • www.willardinter-continental.com • Dis. access • $$$$$*

2 Hay-Adams Hotel

Constructed on the sites of the homes of John Hay and Henry Adams, this elegant hotel features beautifully restored rooms filled with antiques and boasting ornamental ceilings. *16th and H Sts, NW • Map N3 • 202-638-6600 • www.hayadams.com • Dis. access • $$$$*

3 Renaissance Mayflower Hotel

Opened to a huge crowd on the day of Calvin Coolidge's 1925 presidential inauguration, this hotel has been a fixture for politicians – Franklin D. Roosevelt wrote his 1933 inaugural address here and J. Edgar Hoover had lunch here nearly every day. A classic hotel with complimentary shoe shines, and multilingual staff. *1127 Connecticut Ave, NW • Map N3 • 202-347-3000 • www.renaissancemayflower.com • Dis. access • $$$*

4 The Jefferson

The Beaux Arts façade is particularly eye-catching with prints and documents, including some associated with Thomas Jefferson, on display inside. The hotel is a popular choice with celebrities. *16th & M Sts, NW • Map N2 • 202-448-2300 • www.jeffersondc.com • Dis. access • $$$–$$$$*

5 St. Regis Hotel

If both Queen Elizabeth II and the Rolling Stones chose to stay here, the St. Regis must be doing something right. Calvin Coolidge took part in the 1926 opening of this grand hotel, styled after a Renaissance palace and appointed with antiques, chandeliers, and fine tapestries. *923 16th St, NW • Map N2 • 202-638-2626 • www.stregis.com/washington • Dis. access • $$$$*

6 Hotel W

The historic Hotel Washington is now Hotel W, a prestigious property of Starwood Resorts and Hotels. Located next to the White House, many of its rooms have superb views of the White House or the Capitol. Its exceptional service continues in a luxurious setting. *514 15th St, NW • Map P4 • 202-661-2400 • www.whotels.com/washingtondc • Dis. access • $$$$–$$$$$*

7 Morrison-Clark Inn

Created from two townhouses, this mansion served as the Soldiers, Sailors, Marines, and Airmen's Club for 50 years. Decorative touches remain, including four gorgeous mirrors. *1015 L St, NW • Map P3 • 202-898-1200 • www.morrison-clark.com • $$$– $$$$*

8 Phoenix Park Hotel

Named after the famous park in Dublin, this hotel expresses an Irish theme. Built in 1922, the stately Georgian Revival hotel retains an Old World flavor. *520 N Capitol St, NW • Map R4 • 202-638-6900 • www.phoenix-parkhotel.com • Dis. access • $$$–$$$$*

9 Henley Park Hotel

The outside is festooned with gargoyles, and the interior boasts original stained glass. Four-poster beds furnish some rooms. *926 Massachusetts Ave, NW • Map Q3 • 202-638-5200 • www.henleypark.com • Dis. access • $$–$$$*

10 Churchill Hotel

Opened as an apartment building in 1906, this grand hotel provides huge, tastefully furnished rooms with panoramic views. *1914 Connecticut Ave, NW • Map M1 • 202-797-2000 • www.thechurchillhotel.com • Dis. access • $$–$$$*

***Note:** Unless otherwise stated, all hotels accept credit cards, and have en suite bathrooms and air-conditioning*

Above **Mandarin Oriental**

Price Categories

For a standard, double room per night (with breakfast if included), taxes and extra charges.

$	under $100
$$	$100–$200
$$$	$200–$350
$$$$	$350–$500
$$$$$	over $500

Top 10 Luxury Hotels

1 Grand Hyatt Washington

The location is superb and the airy atrium includes a lagoon surrounding an island where a pianist plays. The sports bar is a popular meeting place, and the business center even offers desktop publishing. ⊗ *1000 H St, NW • Map P3 • 202-582-1234 • www.grandhyattwashington.com • Dis. access • $$$*

2 Four Seasons Hotel

This is Washington D.C.'s only five-star hotel. The spa is renowned, and afternoon tea at the Garden Terrace will make any visitor feel special. Convenient to Georgetown and Rock Creek Park. ⊗ *2800 Pennsylvania Ave, NW • Map L3 • 202-342-0444 • www.fourseasons.com/washington • Dis. access • $$$$–$$$$$*

3 Mandarin Oriental Washington, DC

Monumental views over the Potomac Tidal Basin and Jefferson Memorial are plentiful at this elegant hotel. Rooms boast king beds and silk tapestries, as well as luxurious amenities such as plasma TVs and Internet. There is also a fitness center, pool, and spa. ⊗ *1330 Maryland Ave, SW • Map P5 • 202-554-8588 • www.mandarinoriental.com • Dis. access • $$$$–$$$$$*

4 Park Hyatt Washington

The decor at this hotel features original artwork enhancing its elegant ambience. The hotel has an indoor pool and a fitness center. ⊗ *24th St at M St, NW • Map M2 • 202-789-1234 • www.parkwashingtonhyatt.com • Dis. access • $$$$–$$$$$*

5 Gaylord National Resort and Convention Center

South of Washington, the Gaylord National is the largest combined hotel and convention center on the east coast. The 18-story glass atrium offers spectacular views of the Potomac River and Alexandria. ⊗ *201 Waterfront St, National Harbor, MD • Map D6 • 301-965-2000 • www.gaylordhotels.com • $$$*

6 Ritz-Carlton

The Ritz-Carlton provides the finest quality furnishings – Egyptian cotton sheets and down pillows – to make guests comfortable. The marble bathrooms are roomy. Also, traditional pool and fitness and spa facilities. ⊗ *1150 22nd St, NW • Map M3 • 202-835-0500 • www.ritzcarlton.com • Dis. access • $$$$–$$$$$*

7 The Fairfax

The Georgian-style decor here is offset by large LCD TVs, ipod docking and DVD players. Located at a prime Embassy Row location, the hotel attracts diplomats, and also celebrities looking for less conspicuous accommodations. A concierge and a fitness room are available 24 hours a day. ⊗ *2100 Massachusetts Ave, NW • Map M2 • 202-293-2100 • www.luxurycollection.com • Dis. access • $$$$$*

8 Fairmont Washington DC

This hotel's garden courtyard is gorgeous, and a $12 million renovation has made the entire hotel a showplace. Some rooms have delightful balconies. ⊗ *2401 M St, NW • Map M2 • 202-429-2400 • www.fairmont.com • Dis. access • $$$$*

9 Hyatt Regency Washington Capitol Hill

A bustling hotel that takes up an entire block. It is within easy walking distance of the Capitol and the Smithsonian. ⊗ *400 New Jersey Ave at D St, NW • Map R4 • 202-737-1234 • www.hyattregencywashington.com • Dis. access • $$$*

10 The Madison

Located close to the White House, this chic hotel provides comfortable guestrooms, some have covered terraces. Free WiFi throughout. ⊗ *1177 15th St, NW • Map P3 • 202-862-1600 • www.madisonhoteldc.com • Dis. access • $$$–$$$$*

Left and Right **The Latham Hotel**

TOP 10 Moderately Priced Hotels

1 The Latham Hotel

Best known locally as the home of the top-rated Citronelle restaurant *(see p105)*, this is a fine hotel in an excellent Georgetown location. Distinctive two-story carriage suites provide a gracious home base. The poolside patio overlooks the C&O Canal. *3000 M St, NW • Map L2 • 202-726-5000 • www.thelatham.com • $$$*

2 The Normandy Hotel

On a quiet residential street, the Normandy has the feel of a bed-and-breakfast. Complimentary wine and cheese are served Tuesday nights, and coffee, tea, and cookies are offered at other times. *2118 Wyoming Ave, NW • Map M1 • 202-483-1350 • www.doylecollection.com/washington • $$$*

3 The Capitol Hill Suites

This suites-only hotel was re-created from an apartment building, and the result is large spaces with kitchens. Near the Library of Congress, the US Capitol, and Eastern Market. *200 C St, SE • Map S5 • 202-543-6000 • www.capitolhillsuites.com • $$$*

4 Georgetown Inn

This hotel opened in 1961 at the height of the Kennedy administration and the interest in Georgetown glamour, and it has been a fixture ever since. The rooms are large and decorated with style. The Executive Rooms have a sitting area large enough for a meeting, and all rooms have high-speed Internet access. *1310 Wisconsin Ave, NW • Map L2 • 202-333-8900 • www.georgetowninn.com • $$–$$$*

5 Best Western Georgetown Suites

This is a simple downtown hotel, small and relatively quiet, given its popularity with families. The lobby has a working fireplace. All rooms are suites with a separate sitting area and kitchenette. Internet access is included. *1121 New Hampshire Ave, NW • Map M3 • 202-457-0565 • www.bestwesternwashingtondc.com • Dis. access • $$–$$$*

6 Marriott at Metro Center

An excellent downtown location. This smart, modern hotel with 459 rooms and suites still provides a personal touch. The Fire and Sage restaurant has seasonal food. *775 12th St, NW • Map P3 • 202-737-2200 • www.marriott.com • Dis. access • $$$*

7 L'Enfant Plaza Hotel

The Mall is an easy two-block walk from here, and when visitors are not exploring Smithsonian museums, they can enjoy the amenities and fine river views here. There are little TVs in the bathrooms, and an indoor pool. The hotel is also pet friendly. *480 L'Enfant Plaza SW • Map Q5 • 202-484-1000 or 800-235-6397 • www.lenfantplazahotel.com • Dis. access • $$$*

8 Georgetown Suites

Georgetown Suites offers a range of lodging possibilities, all of which have a separate sitting area and a kitchen, and free Wi-Fi. *1000 30th St, NW • Map L3 • 202-298-7800 • www.georgetown suites.com • Dis. access • $$–$$$*

9 Renaissance Washington, DC

This big hotel with over 800 rooms is hard to miss with its striking façade. Oriented toward business travelers, but still a good location in the Penn Quarter. *999 9th St, NW • Map Q3 • 202-898-9000 • www.marriot.com • Dis. access • $$–$$$*

10 Windsor Inn

Two 1920s buildings offer big hotel amenities in a charming environment. The main building is on the National Register of Historic Places, and has some marvelous Art Deco ornamentation. There is no elevator. *1842 16th St, NW • Map N1 • 202-667-0300 • www.windsor-inn-dc.com • $–$$$*

***Note:** Unless otherwise stated, all hotels accept credit cards, and have en suite bathrooms and air-conditioning*

Price Categories

For a standard, double room per night (with breakfast if included), taxes and extra charges.

$	under $100
$$	$100–$200
$$$	$200–$350
$$$$	$350–$500
$$$$$	over $500

Above **The District Hotel**

Top 10 Budget Hotels

1 The District Hotel

This charming old building, about six blocks from the White House, has been converted into 58 rooms that are popular with young people on a limited budget. *1440 Rhode Island Ave, NW • Map P2 • 202-232-7800 • www.districthotel.com • $–$$*

2 State Plaza Hotel

This all-suites hotel, located between the White House and the Kennedy Center, features a bistro with outdoor seating and a rooftop sun deck. Suites come with kitchens and have high-speed Internet connections. *2117 E St, NW • Map M4 • 202-861-8200 • www.stateplaza.com • $$*

3 Adams Inn

A charming urban inn, with 26 rooms. The hotel spreads over three 100-year-old townhouses. Convenient to Adams Morgan and the Zoo. Many rooms share a bath but have a sink in the room. *1746 Lanier Place, NW • Map D3 • 202-745-3600 • www.adamsinn.com • $$*

4 Kalorama Guest House

Spanning architecturally significant townhouses, the Guest House provides a comfortable base in an unbeatable neighborhood. The well maintained rooms are handsomely furnished with plants, Oriental carpets, and period artwork. Continental breakfast is included. *1854 Mintwood Place, NW • Map M1 • 202-667-6369 • www.kaloramaguesthouse.com • $$*

5 Embassy Inn

An elegant apartment house built in 1910 has been converted into a small hotel with 38 guest rooms, all with private bath. The hotel has been modernized, but much of the original decor remains, as do the tasteful façade and entranceway. The furnishings are comfortable reproduction antiques. *1627 16th St, NW • Map N2 • 202-234-7800 • www.embassy-inn-hotel-dc.com • $$*

6 Homewood Suites

This 175-room Hilton is ideal for extended stays as it is centrally located and offers good-sized rooms. Includes gym and Internet. *1475 Massachusetts Ave, NW • Map P2 • 202-265-8000 • www.homewood-suites.com • $$$*

7 The River Inn

This popular Foggy Bottom hotel has 126 suites, each with a full kitchen and a good-sized work or dining area. The name is apt because of the remarkable view of the river, which is bound to put guests in a good mood after a tiring day of sightseeing. *924 25th St, NW • Map M3 • 1-888-874-0100 • www.theriverinn.com • Dis. access • $$–$$$*

8 Donovan House

Located in the center of Downtown Washington, this hotel's decor can be described as minimalist and futuristic. The rooftop bar and pool provide great views of the city. The hotel is pet-friendly. *1155 14th St, NW • Map P3 • 202-737-1200 • www.thompsonhotels.com • Dis. access • $$–$$$*

9 Hotel Harrington

At one time, this was the largest hotel in Washington, and it is still operated by members of the founding family, a century later. Very simple decor and popular with school groups. Has outstanding family suites with two bathrooms. *11th & E Sts, NW • Map P4 • 202-628-8140 • www.hotel-harrington.com • $$*

10 Channel Inn

This hotel is directly on the Southwest Waterfront, with a great view of Washington Channel and Haines Point and a 5-minute walk to the Fish Wharf. The bedrooms have an English-country look with a small balcony. *650 Water St, SW • Map Q6 • 202-554-2400 • www.channelinn.com • Dis. access • $$–$$$*

Left **Holiday Inn Capitol** Right **Swimming pool, Washington Plaza**

TOP 10 Child-Friendly Hotels

1 Holiday Inn Capitol

Outdoor rooftop pool with a view, where kids under 12 eat free, one block from the Air and Space Museum – this combination is hard to beat. The on-site deli provides quick meals and snacks, and there are guest laundry facilities. *550 C St, SW • Map Q5 • 202-479-4000 • www.hicapitoldc.com • Dis. access • $$$*

2 The Liaison Capitol Hill

Previously part of the Holiday Inn chain, this hotel has been well refurbished. The outdoor pool and chests of games and craft activities mean that the little ones will be kept well amused. Under 12s dine free and under 19s stay free. *415 New Jersey Ave, NW • Map R4 • 202-638-1616 • www.affinia.com • Dis. access • $$*

3 Red Roof Inn, Downtown Washington DC

At this hotel there are a multitide of friendly Red Roof family extras: kids can rent video games for in-room play; the TV cable service includes the Cartoon, Discovery, and Learning channels; snack centers relieve the munchies. *500 H St, NW • Map Q3 • 202-289-5959 • www.redroof.com • Dis. access • $$–$$$*

4 Washington Plaza

The beautifully landscaped and resort-like hotel surrounds the big outdoor pool. There is in-room dining and movies. *10 Thomas Circle, NW • Map P2 • 202-842-1300 • www.washingtonplazahotel.com • Dis. access • $$$*

5 J.W. Marriott

Two blocks from the White House, the location minimizes walking distances for little feet. Child care offered by pre-arrangement. *1331 Pennsylvania Ave, NW • Map P4 • 202-393-2000 • www.marriott.com/wasjw • Dis. access • $$$$*

6 Courtyard Washington Northwest

Convenient to the National Zoo *(see pp28–9)*, this hotel provides extra guest-room space and good services. The outdoor pool is safe and fun. Free cookies in the lobby every afternoon. *1900 Connecticut Ave NW • Map M1 • 202-332-9300 • www.marriotthotels.com • Dis. access • $$$*

7 Holiday Inn Central

This downtown hotel has in-room Nintendo game consoles, which, added to the rooftop pool and cable TV and in-room movies, make a pretty complete package for children. Some oversized rooms available. Both Dupont Circle and McPherson Square Metro stops are within walking distance. *1501 Rhode Island Ave at 15th St, NW • Map P2 • 202-483-2000 • www.inn-dc.com • Dis. access • $$*

8 The Quincy Hotel

The decorations here will appeal to urban-oriented kids. In-room movies, treasure chests, sight-seeing books, and pay-to-play Nintendo are offered. *1823 L St, NW • Map N3 • 202-223-4320 • www.thequincy.com • Dis. access • $$–$$$*

9 Washington Suites Georgetown

This excellent Georgetown location provides generous living rooms, large TVs, ipod docking, high speed Internet, and a fully equipped kitchen including a dishwasher. Pets are allowed. *2500 Pennsylvania Ave, NW • Map M3 • 202-333-8060 • www.washingtonsuitesgeorgetown.com • Dis. access • $$*

10 Omni Shoreham Hotel

Close to Rock Creek Park and the National Zoo, this hotel's location makes it ideal for travelers with kids. Young guests are provided with activity backpacks on check-in. *2500 Calvert St, NW (at Connecticut Ave) • Map J5 • 202-234-0700 • www.omnihotels.com • Dis. access • $$$*

***Note:** Unless otherwise stated, all hotels accept credit cards, and have en suite bathrooms and air-conditioning*

Price Categories

For a standard, double room per night (with breakfast if included), taxes and extra charges.	**$** under $100
	$$ $100–$200
	$$$ $200–$350
	$$$$ $350–$500
	$$$$$ over $500

Above **The Inn at Dupont Circle**

TOP 10 Bed-and-Breakfasts

1 Bed-and-Breakfast Accommodations

A reservation service specializing in B&Bs in and around the city. It lists some of the most attractive properties. Staff personally inspect guesthouses on a regular basis. *PO Box 12011, Washington, DC 20005 • 877-893-3233 (Toll free), 202-328-3510 • www.bedandbreakfastdc.com*

2 The Inn at Dupont Circle

This beautiful little inn is a half block from Dupont Circle, and its guests partake of the myriad of restaurants, shops, movie theaters, and art galleries in the neighborhood. The interesting building, with high ceilings and a walled garden, dates from 1855 and once was owned by astrologer Jeanne Dixon. *1312 19th St, NW • Map N2 • 202-467-6777 • www.theinnatdupontcircle.com • $$–$$$*

3 Mansion on O Street

Lavishly decorated, this inn offers a variety of themed rooms, including a Graceland suite filled with memorabilia and the James Bond suite, hidden behind a secret door. The layout is so striking that guests often treat the house as a sight in itself. Eclectic and charming. *2020 O St, NW • Map N2 • 202-496-2000 • www.omansion.com • $$$$$*

4 The Dupont at the Circle

This charming Victorian townhouse offers six comfortable guest rooms and a one-bed apartment. The individually decorated bedrooms are furnished with antiques, and are regularly renovated. *1604 19th St, NW • Map N2 • 202-332-5251 • www.dupontatthecircle.com • $$$*

5 Chester A. Arthur Bed & Breakfast

This handsome and elegantly restored 19th-century townhouse offers over-sized rooms with antiques, cable TV, and Internet access. *13th and P Sts, NW (at Logan Circle) • Map P2 • 877-893-3233 • www.chesterarthurhouse.com • $$–$$$*

6 Swann House

Sometimes described as the best B&B in the city, this charming establishment provides modern conveniences – Wi-Fi, private baths, and cable TV – along with personal attention. *1808 New Hampshire Ave, NW • Map N1 • 202-265-4414 • www.swannhouse.com • $$$*

7 Aaron Shipman House

This classic Victorian mansion, lovingly restored and maintained, is happy to welcome children. Famous for its Christmas decorations. Breakfast – far more elaborate than just "continental" – is served in an elegant dining room. *13th and Q St, NW • Map P2 • 877-893-3233 (Toll free), 202-328-3510 • www.aaronshipmanhouse.com • $–$$*

8 Akwaaba Bed & Breakfast

This elaborately decorated B&B is located within walking distance of the White House. The historic townhouse has eight ensuite rooms, featuring premium linens, cable TV, and CD players. Some rooms have a private balcony, Jacuzzi tub, and a decorative fireplace. *1708 16th St, NW • Map N2 • 866-466-3855 • www.akwaaba.com • $$*

9 The Taft Bridge Inn

Here you'll find 12 beautifully decorated rooms in Victorian style. Near the zoo and the vibrant Adams-Morgan neighborhood. Breakfast included. *2007 Wyoming Ave, NW • Map M1 • 202-387-2007 • www.taftbridgeinn.com • $$*

10 Carriage House

In the heart of Capitol Hill, this B&B is decorated with objects from around the world. It offers four rooms, each with a private bath, TV and complimentary Wi-Fi. Continental-style breakfast is available. *3rd St and South Carolina Ave, SE • Map S6 • 202-328-3510 • www.bedandbreakfastdc.com • $$*

Left and Right **The Hotel George**

TOP 10 Boutique Hotels

1 Topaz Hotel The striking interiors here are in the highest contemporary style along with exquisite design. The Topaz Bar is among the best in the city. Some rooms include yoga and fitness equipment. *1733 N St, NW • Map N2 • 202-393-3000 • www.topazhotel.com • $$$*

2 The Hotel George One of the most fashionable hotels in the city, deserving attention because of its innovative design, excellent business accommodations (the desks are huge slices of granite with contemporary communications), and its fine bistro-style restaurant. The in-room CD player/radio provides sound environments including ocean, brook, forest, or wind. *15 E St, NW • Map R4 • 202-347-4200 • www.hotelgeorge.com • Dis. access • $$$–$$$$*

3 Sofitel Lafayette Square On a corner of Lafayette Square, this 1862 building has been transformed by the French Sofitel chain into an elegant contemporary hotel. The soundproofing and acoustic doors are a welcome feature. The restaurant serves refined French cuisine. *806 15th St, NW • Map P3 • 202-730-8800 • www.sofitelwashingtondc.com • Dis. access • $$$*

4 George Washington University Inn The handsome, large guest rooms and suites of this inn are colonial-inspired, but each come equipped with a refrigerator, microwave, and coffee-maker. Some even have complete kitchens. The Kennedy Center and Metro are nearby. *824 New Hampshire Ave, NW • Map M3 • 1-800-426-4455 • www.gwuinn.com • Dis. access • $$$*

5 Hotel Monticello Mini-suites with refrigerator, microwave, and coffee service are offered at this elegant hotel at one of the best addresses, right up from the C&O canal in Georgetown. The fixtures are beautiful – marble bathrooms and good art on the walls. The service is excellent. *1075 Thomas Jefferson St, NW • Map L3 • 202-337-0900 • www.monticellohotel.com • $$–$$$*

6 Hotel Palomar This funky boutique hotel offers guests luxury accommodation in a lively neighborhood. The rooms in this converted apartment building are large. *2121 P St, NW • Map M2 • 202-448-1800 • www.hotelpalomar-dc.com • $$$*

7 Hotel Lombardy This hotel is decorated with imported fabrics, Oriental rugs, and original art. It is now pet friendly too. The restaurant is bistro-style. *2019 Pennsylvania Ave, NW • Map N3 • 202-828-2600 • www.hotellombardy.com • $$*

8 Hotel Madera Modern comfort with a stylish twist. This small hotel exudes elegance, sophistication, and power, catering to ladies and gentlemen of classic tastes. *1310 New Hampshire Ave, NW • Map N2 • 202-296-7600 • www.hotelmadera.com • $$$*

9 Hotel Monaco Housed in the 19th-century General Post Office building, Hotel Monaco's stately facade conceals a colorful, modern interior. Award-winning on-site restaurant *Poste* provides 24-hour room service. *700 F St, NW • Map Q4 • 202-628-7177 • www.monaco-dc.com • Dis. access • $$-$$$*

10 Melrose Hotel A modern building in a first-rate location at the heart of the city, the Melrose is well known for its refined luxury. The furnishings are contemporary but with classic influences. *2430 Pennsylvania Ave, NW • Map M3 • 202-955-6400 • www.melrosehoteldc.com • Dis. access • $$$*

Note: *Unless otherwise stated, all hotels accept credit cards, and have en suite bathrooms and air-conditioning*

Price Categories

For a standard, double room per night (with breakfast if included), taxes and extra charges.	
$	under $100
$$	$100–$200
$$$	$200–$350
$$$$	$350–$500
$$$$$	over $500

Above **Typical Washington, D.C. business hotel lobby**

Top 10 Business Hotels

1 Marriott Wardman Park

The largest convention hotel in Washington combines charm with modern services and technology. There are scores of meeting rooms here and an exhibition area. The well-maintained rooms offer all business services. *2660 Woodley Rd, NW • Map J5 • 202-328-2000 • www.marriott.com • Dis. access • $$$–$$$$*

2 Crystal City Marriott

This hotel has good business amenities and is convenient to the Pentagon and within a mile of Reagan National Airport. There are 13 meeting rooms and a walkway to a shopping mall. *1999 Jefferson Davis Highway, Arlington VA • Map D4 • 703-413-5500 • www.marriott.com • $$$*

3 Omni Shoreham Hotel

Adjacent to Rock Creek Park, this grand hotel sits on 11 landscaped acres. A dynamic, luxury hotel that has hosted countless important guests and meetings. The full business center also includes clerical support. Multiple large meeting rooms. *2500 Calvert St, NW (near Connecticut Ave) • Map J5 • 202-234-0700 • www.omnihotels.com • Dis. access • $$$*

4 Hamilton Crowne Plaza Hotel

This is a distinguished hotel, where the guest rooms offer a desk with high-speed Internet and voice mail, and cable TV with in-room movies. Fourteen meeting rooms are available with teleconferencing and a multilingual staff. Pets are welcome. *14th and K St, NW • Map P3 • 202-682-0111 • www.hamiltondchotel.com • $$$*

5 Embassy Suites

Well-furnished rooms with good work areas and a separate living room for meetings or relaxing. Conference rooms with extensive equipment available for rent. Indoor swimming pool and fitness center. Part of the Hilton group. *1250 22nd St, NW • Map M2 • 202-857-3388 • www.washingtondc.embassysuites.com • Dis. access • $$$*

6 One Washington Circle Hotel

Business travelers receive excellent services at this Foggy Bottom hotel. A knowledgable staff manages the five meeting rooms, and suites have lots of seating space for work. Larger suites have full kitchens and walk-out balconies. There is also an outdoor pool. *1 Washington Circle, NW • Map M3 • 202-872-1680 • www.thecirclehotel.com • $$$*

7 Capital Hilton

A huge range of meeting rooms and guest rooms with desks and modern communications. *1001 16th St at K St, NW • Map N3 • 202-393-1000 • www.hilton.com • Dis. access • $$$–$$$$*

8 Four Points by Sheraton

Business facilities as well as Wi-Fi, an indoor pool, and fitness center. *1201 K St, NW • Map P3 • 202-289-7600 • www.fourpoints.com • Dis. access • $$$*

9 Hilton Washington

The garden setting is lovely, and the elevated location gives a good view of the skyline. Both the layout and size of this complex create a resort atmosphere, while staff and facilities offer every amenity. *1919 Connecticut Ave, NW • Map N1 • 202-483-3000 • www.washington.hilton.com • Dis. access • $$$–$$$$*

10 Courtyard Washington Convention Center

Situated in an old 1891 bank but completely up-to-date, and with an indoor pool and fitness center. The hotel has two conference rooms. *900 F St NW • Map Q4 • 202-638-4600 • www.courtyard.com/wascn • Dis. access • $$$*

General Index

Acknowledgments

Main Contributors
Ron Burke is the author or co-author of 19 books. A former Capitol Hill resident, he was born in the Washington, DC metropolitan area and has lived here most of his life.

Susan Burke lives in Virginia, where she worked on a daily newspaper for 20 years before becoming an editor for the Air Line Pilots Association. She is also a freelance editor for journals on labor, economics, and art conservation.

Produced by Sargasso Media Ltd, London

Project Editor Zoë Ross
Art Editor Philip Lord
Picture Research Helen Stallion
Proofreader Stewart J Wild
Indexer Hilary Bird
Editorial Assistance Ebba Tinwin

Main Photographer Scott Suchman

Additional Photography
Phillipe Dewet, Paul Franklin, Kim Sayer, Giles Stokoe

Illustrator chrisorr.com

FOR DORLING KINDERSLEY
Publishing Manager Marisa Renzullo
Publisher Douglas Amrine
Senior Cartographic Editor Casper Morris
Senior DTP Jason Little
Production Melanie Dowland
Picture Librarians Hayley Smith, David Saldanha
Maps John Plumer

Revisions Team
Emma Anacootee, Shruti Bahl, Tessa Bindloss, Sherry Collins, Anne Coombes, Imogen Corke, Nicola Erdpresser, Karen Fitzpatrick, Calum Forsyth, Rhiannon Furbear, Prerna Gupta, Lydia Halliday, Christine Heilman, Rose Hudson, Integrated Publishing Solutions, Claire Jones, Juliet Kenny, Carly Madden, Alison McGill, Sonal Modha, Vikki Nousiainen, Catherine Palmi, Pollyanna Poulter, Melanie Renzulli, Lucy Richards, Meredith Smith, Susana Smith, Litta W. Sanderson, Brett Steel, Lauren Thomas, Conrad Van Dyk, Karen Villabona, Hugo Wilkinson

Picture Credits
a-above; b-below/bottom; c-centre; f-far; l-left; r-right; t-top.

The publishers would like to thank the following individuals, companies and picture libraries for their kind permission to reproduce their photographs:

2 AMYS: 113tc; ALAMY: Ghostwork Images/Wm. Baker, 82tl; ALLSPORT: 61r; ASTORINO PHOTOGRAPHICS INC. Alexandria, Virginia: 83tl. CORBIS: 4–5, 6t, 8b, 8–9, 10tl, 10tr, 10b, 32t, 36tl, 36tr, 36c, 36b, 37l, 37r, 38tl, 38tr, 38c, 38b, 39l, 39tr, 39br, 54tl, 55r, 65r, 80–81, 96tr, 102–103, 106tl, 110–11, 114–15. FREER GALLERY OF ART, Smithsonian Institution, Washington DC: 41c; GREEN PAPAYA: 113tl; Courtesy of the HERITAGE SMITHSONIAN INSTITUTION: 64tl; Christine Parker 64b. LEONARDO MEDIABANK:130tl; LIBRARY OF CONGRESS: 25t; THE MONOCLE: 75tc; Courtesy of the MOUNT VERNON LADIES' ASSOCIATION: 7t,

32bl, 32br, 32–3, 33c, 64tl. NATIONAL AIR AND SPACE MUSEUM: 16c, 17ca; NATIONAL BUILDING MUSEUM: Liz Roll, 72tr; NATIONAL CHERRY BLOSSOM FESTIVAL: 64tr; ©2009 Board of Trustees, NATIONAL GALLERY OF ART, Washington: Fra Angelico & Filippo Lippi, *The Adoration of the Magi*, c1445, Samuel H. Kress Collection: 20b; John Constable, *Wivenhoe Park*, 1816, Widener Collection: 21t; Leonardo da Vinci, *Ginevra de Benci*, Ailsa Mellon Bruce Fund: 20cl; Frans Hals, *Portrait of an Elderly Lady*, 1633, Winslow Homer *Right and Left*, 1909. Gift of the Avalon Foundation 21cr; Andrew W. Mellon Collection: 22b; Claude Monet, *The Japanese Footbridge*, 1899, Gift of Victorian Mebeker Coberly, in memory of her son John W. Mudd, and Walter H. and Leonore Annenburg: 22tc; Maurice Brazil Prendegast, *Salem Cove*, 1916, Collection of Mr and Mrs Paul Mellon: 22tl; *Graft*, 2008-2009 Roxy Paine, Gift of Victoria and Roger Sant 23br; Gilbert Stuart, *George Washington*, c1821, Gift of Thomas Jefferson Coolidge IV, in Memory of his Great Grand-father, Thomas Jefferson Coolidge, His Grandfather, Thomas Jefferson Coolidge II and his Father, Thomas Jefferson Coolidge III: 7cl, 21b; Johannes Vermeer, *Girl with the Red Hat*, Andrew W. Mellon Collection: 20cr; NATIONAL MUSEUM OF AMERICAN HISTORY/ SMITHSONIAN INSTITUTION: 6br, 18c, 18b, 19c, Richard Strauss 19tr, designed by James Galanos 19bl; NATIONAL PARK SERVICE: Abbie Row 15; NORTHWEST FLOWER AND GARDEN SHOW: 65tl. NEWSEUM: 86cr; THE PARK AT FOURTEENTH: Jim Lollard 62tr; PARK HYATT WASHINGTON: 97tc; SMITHSONIAN INSTITUTION: Eric Long 83tr; SMITHSONIAN NATIONAL ZOOLOGICAL PARK: Jessie Cohen: 28t, 28bl, 29t, 29cr, 29cl; Meghan Murphy 28–9c. US CAPITOL HISTORICAL SOCIETY: 9cr, 9b. VERIDIAN SYSTEMS DIVISION: 17cb. WHITE HOUSE COLLECTION, COURTESY WHITE HOUSE HISTORICAL TRUST: 12b, 12– 13, 13t, 13cb, 13b, 14tl, 14tr, 14b; Bruce White 6bl.

All other images are © Dorling Kindersley. For further information see *www.dkimages.com*

Selected Street Index

1st Street NE R4
1st Street NW R4
1st Street SE R5
1st Street SW R5
2nd Street NE S4
2nd Street NW R4
2nd Street SE S5
2nd Street SW R5
3rd Street NE S4
3rd Street NW R4
3rd Street SE S5
3rd Street SW R5
4th Street NE S4
4th Street NW Q4
4th Street SE S6
4th Street SW Q5
5th Street NE S4
5th Street NW Q4
5th Street SE Q5
6th Street NE S4
6th Street NW Q4
6th Street SE S6
6th Street SW Q5
7th Street NE S4
7th Street NW Q4
7th Street SE S6
7th Street SW Q5
8th Street NW Q4
9th Street NW Q4
9th Street SW Q5
10th Street NW P4
10th Street SW P5
11th Street NW P4
12th Street NW P3
12th Street SW P5
13th Street NW P4
13th Street SW P5
14th Street NW P4
14th Street SW P5
15th Street NW P4
15th Street SW P5
16th Street NW N3
17th Street NW N4
18th Street NW N4
19th Street NW N4
20th Street NW N4
21st Street NW M4
22nd Street NW M4
23rd Street NW M4
24th Street NW M4
25th Street NW M4
26th Street NW M4
27th Street NW M3
28th Street NW L2
29th Street NW L2
30th Street NW L2
31st Street NW L2
32nd Street NW L1
33rd Street NW L2
34th Street NW K2
35th Street NW K2
36th Street NW K2
37th Street NW K2
38th Street NW K1
44th Street NW G3
A Street NE S4
A Street SE S5
Adams Mill Road J4
Albemarle Street H3
Arlington Boulevard K4
Broad Branch Road H1
C Street NE S4
C Street NW Q4
C Street SE S5
C Street SW Q5
Calvert Street J5
Canal Road NW K2
Canal Street NW K3
Cathedral Avenue G4
Chevy Chase Circle G1
Church Street NW P2
Cleveland Avenue H4
Columbia Road NW N1
Connecticut Avenue NW N2
Constitution Avenue NE S4
Constitution Avenue NW Q4
D Street NE S4
D Street NW Q4
D Street SE R5
D Street SW Q5
Daniel French Drive SW M5
Delaware Avenue NE R4
Delaware Avenue SW R6
Dumbarton Street NW L2
Dupont Circle N2
Dwight D Eisenhower Freeway Q6
E Street NE S4
E Street NW Q4
E Street SE S6
E Street SW Q6
East Basin Drive SW N5
Ellipse Road NW N4
Executive Avenue NW N4
F Street NE S4
F Street NW Q4
F Street SE S6
Farragut Square N3
Florida Avenue NE S2
Florida Avenue NW R2
Folger Square S5
Foxhall Road G6
Franklin Square P3
Freedom Plaza P4
Fulton Street G5
G Street NE S3
G Street NW R3
G Street SE S6
G Street SW Q6
George Washington Memorial Parkway K4
Georgia Avenue NW Q1
Grace Street NW L3
H Street NE S3
H Street NW R3
Henry Bacon Drive NW M5
I (Eye) Street NE R3
I (Eye) Street NW Q3
I (Eye) Street SE R6
I (Eye) Street SW Q6
Idaho Avenue G4
Independence Avenue SE R5
Independence Avenue SW Q5
Indiana Avenue NW Q4
Jefferson Davis Highway L5
Jefferson Drive SW Q5
K Street NE S3
K Street NW Q3
K Street SE S6
K Street SW R6
L Street NE R3
L Street NW Q3
L Street SE S6
Lafayette Square N3
Linnean Avenue H2
Logan Circle P2
Louisiana Avenue NW R4
Lovers Lane Walkway NW L1
M Street NE S2
M Street NW R2
MacArthur Boulevard G6
Macomb Street H4
Madison Drive NW P5
Maine Avenue SW Q6
Market Square Q4
Maryland Avenue SW Q5
Massachusetts Avenue NE S4
Massachusetts Avenue NW Q3
McPherson Square P3
Memorial Drive L5
Military Road G2
Mount Vernon Square Q3
N Street NE R2
N Street NW Q2
Nebraska Avenue NW H2
New Hampshire Avenue NW M2
New Jersey Avenue NW R4
New Jersey Avenue SE R5
New Mexico Avenue G4
New York Avenue NW Q3
North Capitol Street R3
O Street NW R2
Ohio Drive N6
Olive Street NW L2
P Street NE R2
P Street NW Q2
Park Road J3
Pennsylvania Avenue NW P4
Pennsylvania Avenue SE S5
Porter Street H4
Prospect Street NW K2
Q Street NW Q2
R Street NW Q1
Reno Road H3
Reservoir Road G6
Rhode Island Avenue NW N2
River Road G2
Rock Creek & Potomac Parkway M4
Rock Creek Parkway L1
S Street NW R1
Scott Circle N2
Seward Square S5
Sheridan Circle M2
South Capitol Street R5
South Street NW L3
Stanton Square S4
T Street NW R1
Tenley Circle G3
Thomas Circle P2
Thomas Jefferson Street NW L3
Tilden Street H3
Tunlaw Road G5
U Street NW R1
Utah Avenue H1
V Street NW R1
Van Ness Street G3
Vermont Avenue NW P2
Virginia Avenue NW M4
Volta Place NW K2
W Street NW R1
Ward Circle G4
Washington Avenue SW R5
Washington Circle M3
Water Street SW Q6
West Basin Drive SW N5
Western Avenue G1
Whitehaven Parkway NW K1
Whitehurst Freeway NW L3
Wisconsin Avenue NW L2
Yuma Street G3